SUSSEX

WALKS FOR MOTORISTS

Douglas Lasseter

30 Walks with sketch maps

GW00598182

COUNTRYSIDE BOOKS
NEWBURY, BERKSHIRE

Countryside Books' walking guides cover most areas of England and Wales and include the following series:

County Rambles
Walks for Motorists
Exploring Long Distance Paths
Literary Walks
Pub Walks

A complete list is available from the publishers.

First published 1992
© Douglas Lasseter 1992

COUNTRYSIDE BOOKS
3 Catherine Road
Newbury, Berkshire

ISBN 1 85306 170 0

Sketch Maps by the Author

Cover photograph: South Downs Way above Alfriston
taken by Bill Meadows

Publishers' Note

At the time of publication all footpaths used in these walks were designated as official footpaths or rights of way, but it should be borne in mind that diversion orders may be made from time to time.

Although every care has been taken in the preparation of this Guide, neither the Author nor the Publisher can accept responsibility for those who stray from the Rights of Way.

Typeset by Acorn Bookwork, Salisbury, Wiltshire
Produced through MRM Associates Ltd., Reading
Printed in England by J.W. Arrowsmith Ltd., Bristol

Contents

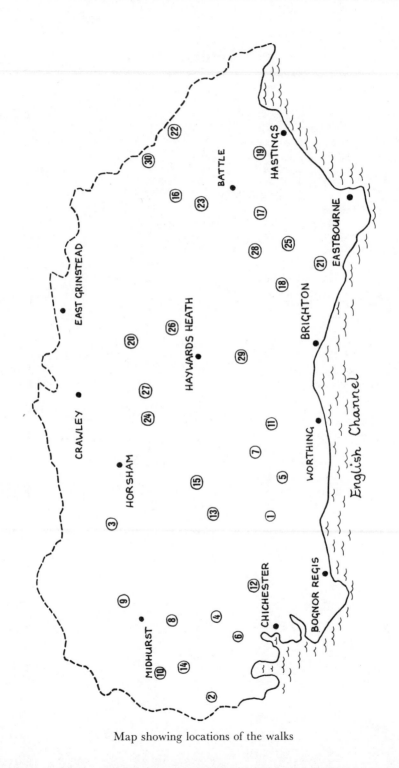

Map showing locations of the walks

To my wife for her companionship and help on these walks, my daughter for her hard work under difficult circumstances, our friends and co founding members of:

'The Sussex Wayfarers'

But especially to Alexander who still has 28 to go!

Introduction

These walks range the whole considerable length of Sussex and, in compiling this book, as with all our many other walking activities, my wife and myself (observing the philosophy of that intrepid 18th century Englishman Dr Johnson), travelled 'hopefully'. In our case, however, we have the certain expectation that around every bend along the way, old or new to us, there will be some surprise to delight us, as surely, dear reader, there will be for you. Even a well loved route, rewalked at a different time of day, or year, or in a different direction, will offer some new surprise in this beautiful county of ours.

All the walks are circular, starting and finishing at the same point. All have adequate parking, but *please* take care not to cause an obstruction, particularly to farm traffic. Each walk has particular points of interest to intrigue you – notwithstanding their beautiful natural surroundings. With the exception of one walk (and that you must find out for yourself) all have a pub or some other refreshment establishment along the route, or very close by. Indeed, some of the more remote pubs can be of considerable architectural and historical interest. Who knows, you may even enjoy the bonus, on a summer weekday evening, of hearing Sussex countrymen engaged in countryside talk!

You will find that none of these walks are qualified with a time in which they can be done. Even with the shorter walks (possibly those in particular), they contain so much of interest that they will take as long as the time which is available to you. Certainly not for us, and we hope not for you, the fetish practised by many so called 'Rambling Clubs', whose aim appears to be record breaking between points A and B. 'Did you see those orchids?' – 'What orchids?'

In planning your day, a rule of thumb to gauge distance vs time is very simple: you will cover 2 – 2.5 mph at a steady walking pace. But conversely, for instance, walk number 23 – Brightling and Mad Jack Fuller's Follies – a distance of less than 4 miles and with so much of interest, could take a half day or more.

We have taken particular care to ensure the accuracy of the text directions and their accompanying sketch maps. All the routes are over public rights of way, the exception being Arundel Park, where one has the 'right to roam'. Each walk quotes the relevant Ordnance Survey sheet number of the particular area together with the starting point grid reference numbers thus:

> (187) = OS Landranger series, scale 1 : 50.000
> Sheet number 187, 'Dorking, Reigate and Crawley area'.
> (187) 347294 = the village car park location in Ardingly, the starting point of Walk 20.

All Landranger series maps have a short explanation on how to calculate a grid reference point. The relevant maps in the OS Pathfinder series, scale 1 : 25.000 are also quoted. Whilst claiming the accuracy of the information, I would nevertheless recommend that it is wise to arm yourself with the relevant OS sheet. Should you, therefore, stray beyond the confines of our sketch maps, you will be able to relocate yourself back onto the correct route.

Sussex does not have particularly 'hard' walking conditions, but you are advised to be well shod as some of the footpaths and tracks can be quite rough and stony. In places even on the sunniest day there will be mud! Having lightweight (inexpensive) rain resistant clothing with you can save considerable discomfort from both wind and rain, and we would not want you to be discouraged by an easily preventable 'bad' experience. Likewise, it is quite easy to carry some emergency rations in the form of biscuits, chocolate bars and a flask of water or juice – or whatever you fancy . . . This precaution will stave off those long forgotten hunger and thirst pangs brought on by fresh air and exercise.

Please observe the Country Code, in general by taking all your food wrappers, containers and cans back home with you for proper disposal and, in particular, positively ensuring that you secure all gates behind you. You will be pleased to know that well behaved, controlled dogs are welcome in the countryside.

One term frequently used throughout this book which might require explanation is 'field headland'. It is the countryman's term for 'the edge of a field' that is bordered by a hedge, stream, fence, lane etc. You will recall that I say that all these walks are over 'public rights of way' and without exception that is the case, you may occasionally, however, be confronted by a notice claiming that the way ahead is 'Private, No Entry' and on closer inspection you will find that much smaller print will confirm 'Footpath and Bridleway only, no entry for cars'. This is the owner's quite justifiable means of keeping intruding motorists at bay, and you may proceed on the intended route in such cases.

So, dear Reader, here you are, suitably kitted out, provisioned and advised – ready to set out and enjoy these walks.

Douglas Lasseter
Spring 1992

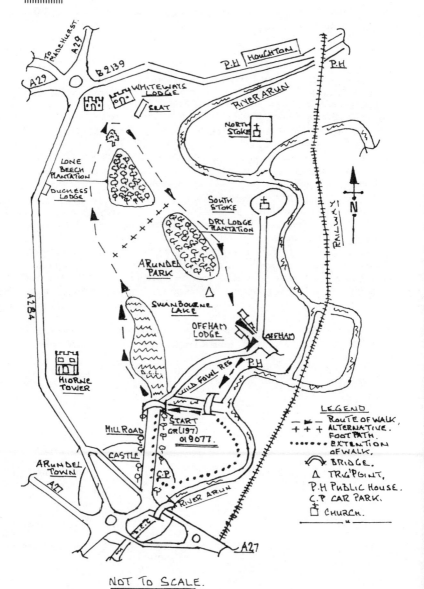

NOT TO SCALE.

ARUNDEL PARK

★

4.6 miles (6.2 km)
or
6.2 miles (9.9 km)

Maps 1 : 50.000 scale 197. 1 : 25.000 scale TQ 00/10 and 01/11

The fame of this 'ancient and grandly historical town' must be worldwide, and it is undoubtedly a tourist trap, but I wonder how many visitors appreciate just how close they are to the 1,200 acres of delight contained in its Park, or the panoramic views to be marvelled at within a mile's walk of the entrance gates to Swanbourne Lake.

It is a sad fact that the origins and the originator of the castle are not known, but nevertheless many prominent figures in history have been associated with it, including William Rufus, Earl Godwin and his son Harold, and Henry I, who seized the place from the then Earl Marshal of England, Roger de Montgomeri, and 'gave' Arundel to his brother, Hugh. All this and more can be gleaned from a tour of the castle, which is open April 1st—October 26th daily except Saturdays.

Having reached the head of Swanbourne Lake, the walk then climbs quite gently to attain an elevation of 408 ft (124 m) in about a mile, at a point quite close to Whiteways Lodge. The track then swings round almost in a reciprocal direction to descend and exit from the Park at Offham Lodge Gates, from where the walk joins the river Arun bank path.

Arundel is situated off the A27, midway between Worthing to the east and Chichester to the west and 4 miles north of Littlehampton. There is adequate parking in the town with some car parks free, or on reduced tariff during the winter months (October–March). However, this walk is designed to start from the south side of the Mill Stream Bridge at the end of Mill Road (leading to the *Black Rabbit* pub) with this lovely road being bordered on either side by lime trees. The east side of this entire stretch of road has free on-road parking all year round, with the start of the walk at GR(197)019077.

Having crossed (north) over the Mill Stream Bridge, turn left into the signposted footpath which leads through a stile over a timber causeway and on to the south side lake path, which continues now to the head of the lake. On reaching it, turn right (to the north shore path) then left, going over a cattle grid and through a gate at a footpath sign. The broad grassy valley path will go by a three-way footpath sign on the left. Continue ahead to reach, in only a short distance, another three-way footpath sign but walk on through the valley. (*Note*, this is the area of the Park used at one time as a firing range though it is no longer used for that purpose. However, an occasional pheasant shoot is held here and should the walker encounter this, then simply turn right at the footpath sign to go through a gate and continue uphill, alongside the training gallops where at the top of the hill the path joins the track from Whiteways Lodge, at the northern end of Dry Lodge Plantation).

The wide, ascending valley floor path will, in under a mile, reach a large solitary oak tree. Shortly beyond it will meet a metalled track, which to the left goes through a gate to Duchess Lodge. Our route is to the right and shortly the track surface reverts to stone and you will encounter a bend. On the left is a Victorian park seat. Bear off now to the right; there is also a solitary beech tree at this position. Walk ahead on the track, which now commands panoramic views of the Arun valley (Amberley Vale) to the left which will continue to unfold, even to the point where the continuing track drops down to Offham. On the right the track continues by the replanted area of Lone Beech Plantation, devastated by the 1987 October hurricane. The stony track goes through a gate but now becomes a wide, well defined downland path which will head directly for Dry Lodge Plantation. As you approach it you will see the footpath sign over to the right which you would encounter if you had been diverted by a pheasant shoot as mentioned earlier.

The path continues by the plantation on the right, whilst on the left views of North and South Stoke are seen. Go through another gate and just beyond, the path makes a fork—bear now into the right-hand branch, with the plantation still continuing on the right. Go through a third gate. The now stony track starts to descend almost immediately. Over to the right a trig. point will be in sight. In only a few yards, the track will meet with another coming from the right, bear left onto it. This rough stony track has a high grass bank on the left and in order to keep the views in sight longer, and to make the walking easier, go to the top of the bank and continue along on its downland turf top.

You will, of course, be forced back onto the track just before reaching the farm buildings and Offham Lodge Gate, known locally as the Lion and Unicorn Gate. Sadly the unicorn has been vandalised and is now missing its horn.

Once through the gate, come out onto the Offham/South Stoke road and walk straight ahead. Come next to a junction in the lane, where you should note that the way ahead—signposted to Offham—is not a public right of way. Turn right into the high banked lane which will shortly reach the old quarrymen's cottages on the right, with the north aspect of the *Black Rabbit* pub on the left.

Depending upon the time of day and the ability (or not as the case may be) to resist the delights of the *Black Rabbit* , the walk continues just beyond the entrance road to the pub and will come to the old disused Offham Chalk Quarry on the right, opposite which is a steel gate and stile. Go over it and bear right on the river Arun bank path. This will pass by on the right the fenced area of the Wildfowl Reserve Wet Lands—Arundel Castle is now in full view. Go by the next footpath sign on the right and cross over the double stiles and bridgeway over the mill stream outfall into the Arun. Now immediately on the right is a three-way footpath sign and another stile which is the shorter way back on the south mill stream bank path to Mill Road.

However, hopefully well fortified from the visit to the *Black Rabbit*, you may continue along by the river bank path which will exit into the Mill Road car park, and walk down the beautiful tree-lined avenue of Mill Road to rejoin your car. This is the additional distance of 1.6 miles.

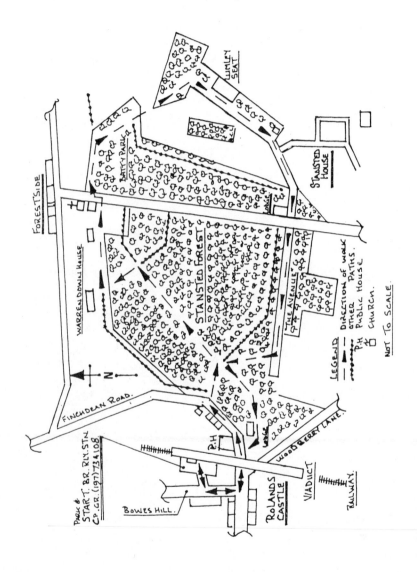

STANSTED FOREST AND STANSTED HOUSE

WALK 2

★

5 miles (8 km)

Maps 1 : 50.000 scale 197. 1 : 25.000 scale SU61/71

The parking place for this walk, Rolands Castle BR car park, is in Hampshire, whilst the area of the walk is in West Sussex. Rolands Castle village is a very attractive place with the large village green as its centrepiece, bordered by houses, shops, post office and two pubs—almost next door to each other. During the 17th and 18th centuries it was a notorious centre of smuggling, and it appears that a major feature of the frequent clashes between smugglers and 'Preventors' was throwing each other down local wells!

A feature recommended for this walk is a visit to magnificent Stansted House, open to the public between May 5th and September 25th: Sunday, Monday and Tuesdays only. The estate is now administered by the Stansted Park Foundation (0705) 412265, but the house is still used by the Bessborough family. These dates notwithstanding, my wife and I walked this lovely forest and farmland route during the winter of 1991. The woods were alive with many species of birds. We had a close encounter with two does and saw a number of other deer as well as a fox—altogether a delightful walk in all seasons, on good paths and tracks over gentle undulating countryside.

There are good roads to this venue from the south via the A27(T) from Southbourne and Emsworth. When approaching the village from this direction, you should take care in negotiating the viaduct beyond which you turn right into Boweshill, the road leading to the railway station. Alternatively, there is good access from the A3(T) and from this direction you travel eastwards through the village then turn left into Boweshill, just before going under the viaduct. The parking and starting location for this walk is the BR car park at Rowlands Castle at GR(197)734108 with free (1991) parking.

Leave the car park and walk down to the road and turn left to go under the viaduct; you are now in Finch Dean Road. A few yards beyond the viaduct, pass the pub and houses on the left to reach shortly, on the same side, a pair of flint and brick houses.

On the opposite side of the road are the signs of the Hampshire and West Sussex boundary markers, and set into the wall there is the entrance into Stansted Forest. Cross the road, go through the gateway, and on your left will be a three-way sign; walk straight ahead to a clearing with a stand of beech trees. Walk on a few yards to reach a stone surface track on the other side of which is another three-way sign (the point of your return). Turn left onto this track.

13

In only a few hundred yards on the left, will be a turning going up to a cottage. Continue on to a fork in the track, turn into the left hand branch. On your left will be the stump remains of a footpath signpost whilst on the right and secured to a tree trunk, a notice-board with the message '*Game Reserve. Footpath to Forestside. All persons are requested to keep to the footpath*'. After some distance, the forest track will make a junction with a wide grass firebreak; on the left will be a two-way sign. Turn left here and in only a few feet to your right, will be another two-way sign. Turn right onto the continuing forest track, which will come to another wide grass firebreak. Cross it and with a two-way sign on your right, walk on. Cross over another forest track, to reach yet another firebreak and passing a further footpath sign (also on the right)—walk on. Next you come to a three-way sign, still on the right; walk on a few yards to a second three-way sign and here turn left. This new direction will lead to, in a few yards, a very old, many-trunked yew tree, which the path goes around. The yew will be on your right, whilst on the left is a fairly deep depression in the ground. The path will now descend through the woods to a stile with a footpath sign at the edge of a narrow open pasture field; go over this stile to cross another on the other side of the field. Warren Down House is now in full view. Shortly beyond the second stile is a three-way sign; turn right and continue up this narrow path which will make a junction with the driveway into Warren Down House. Turn right onto it—there is a two-way sign here.

This wide track now continues and will pass by Forestside Farm, on the left, to make a junction with the Forestside Road. Turn left onto it, passing on the left the houses of this hamlet and you will very shortly reach 'Christ's Church of Forestside', a 19th century building which is usually open should you care to visit it. Just beyond the church, and on the right, is a gate and stile with a footpath sign; go over the stile. The path is going now into the woods of Batty Park; it will continue and turn right to have the hedge on the left. Passing by an iron Victorian kissing-gate set in the hedge, continue past a stile and three-way sign on the left, coming then to an opposing hedge where there is another iron kissing-gate and three-way sign; turn right.

In about a hundred yards, this new path will reach a three-way sign. Walk on by it. Again, in only a very short distance come to a two-way sign and turn left, passing on the left another two-way sign. Continue straight ahead and in about 20 yards come to a crossing track and a two-way sign. Carry straight on—this path is now going through Wythypiece Woods.

The path will then come to a small clearing. On the left is a three-way sign; opposite to it is another three-way sign—cross over the small clearing and turn left, the second three-way sign is now on your right. This leads shortly to a two-way sign (also on the right); now turn right. Go over a stile into a cultivated field—across this field is a copse and in clear view on its edge is a footpath sign; walk across the field to it. With the sign and the edge of this copse on your left (ie having turned right), continue around the copse coming to another footpath sign. Shortly beyond this is a very large solitary oak tree. With this also on your left, walk on the next few yards where, set in the corner of the field, is a stile. Go over it and follow the footpath sign direction through this narrow section of woods. You will now see the house called Lumley Seat. The woodland path then makes a junction with a metalled lane, turn right onto it.

Passing Lumley Seat on the left, the lane will continue and will reach a large mellowed building on the left. Go through a gate and turn right (still on the metalled lane), where shortly beyond is a junction going off to the left which will take you to Stansted House—now in full view. What an impressive sight it is! If you have planned your day to include a visit to the house (during the open season), then you may use this approach drive, but during the closed periods this is not a right of way. Whatever your choice, continue the walk in your original direction down the metalled lane, which will reach the equally impressive structure of Stansted's Eastern Lodge Gate. Go across the Forestside Road, making sure to go through the iron kissing-gate on the opposite side—not the timber gate to the right. You will now be walking down 'The Avenue'—the original carriageway between Rolands Castle and Stansted House. This very wide tree-lined avenue, over a mile long stretch of beautiful greensward, must be the most impressive in the whole county if not the country. What a marvellous sight. Pause occasionally and look back at the house, seeming not to diminish at all with distance.

Eventually the carriageway is blanked off by a line of trees. Walk to the right hand corner, go through a gap and turn left onto a descending track which will shortly bring you to the stone-surfaced track and the three-way sign of the start of this walk. Here turn left and walk the short distance to Stansted House's Western Lodge Gate—go out onto the road (Woodberry Lane). The viaduct now towers above you, and it is only a short distance back to your car—after a successful and satisfying day.

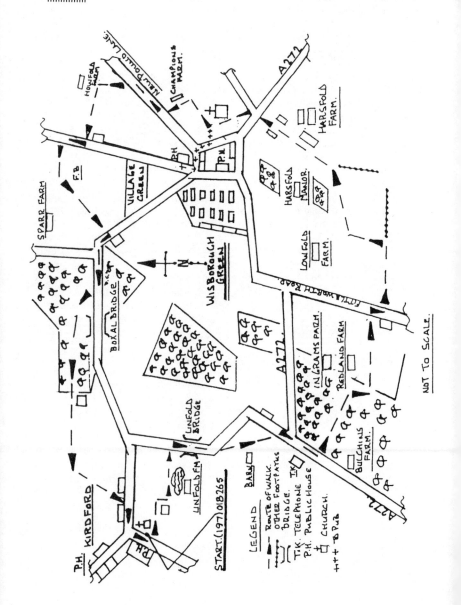

WALK 3

NEW POUND LANE

CHAMPIONS FARM.

A272

HARSFOLD FARM.

HOWFOLD FARM

HARSFOLD MANOR.

P.H.

P.H.

SPARR FARM

F.B.

VILLAGE GREEN

LOWFOLD FARM.

WISBOROUGH GREEN

N

BOXAL BRIDGE

A272

INGRAMS PATH

REDLAND FARM

FITTLEWORTH ROAD

UNFOLD BRIDGE

UNFOLD FM.

BULCHINS FARM.

A272

P.H. KIRDFORD

P.H.

BARN

START: (197) 018265

LEGEND
---- ROUTE OF WALK.
——— OTHER FOOTPATHS
++++ BRIDGE.
T.K. TELEPHONE   T.K.
P.H. PUBLIC HOUSE
✚ CHURCH.
+++ TB PUB

NOT TO SCALE.

KIRDFORD AND WISBOROUGH GREEN

WALK 3

★

8.5 miles (13.6 km)

Maps 1 : 50.000 scale 197. 1 : 25.000 scale TQ 02/12

One of the longer, all day, walks in West Sussex, this is nonetheless over gently undulating terrain across farmland and through woodland and it really does make a lovely day out. The paths and tracks are mainly good underfoot, even in winter. With the route of the walk going by the churches of both Kirdford and Wisborough Green, I recommend that you visit both these lovely old buildings. The latter especially as it contains a specially commissioned tapestry designed by a local artist, Patrick Gierth and worked by the ladies of the village to commemorate the particular relationship this village had with the Canadian Forces during the Second World War, and is really worth a visit.

Kirdford lies north-east of Petworth and about 5 miles from it via Balls Cross off the A283 road from Petworth. Alternatively, coming from the east and taking the cross country A272 road, turn off north after leaving Wisborough Green and the unlisted road is signposted to Kirdford. The parking and starting location of this walk is opposite *The Half Moon* pub in Kirdford and just a short way north of the church. The on-road parking on this quiet village road is quite safe, even on a Sunday, but please do not park in the small service road area of the adjacent houses. GR(197)018265.

Going through the church lychgate, go on past the front of the church and turn left onto the path beyond. This is a public footpath coming from the road. Walk the length of the churchyard, go over a stile at the end and turn right onto the signposted path. Only a short way ahead and going over another stile, with a hedge on your right, walk on towards barns and other farm buildings in front of you. On reaching these buildings, walk around them as directed by the two footpath signs and with a building on the right, the path leads to a stile set in a hedge. Go over it and turn left and you now have a hedge on your left. In front of you at the other end of the field is a gateway and two-way sign and on reaching it go over a cattle grid. On the other side turn sharp right into a woodland path at the end of which, at a two-way sign, go over a stile. You are now on the driveway to Linfold Farm, the buildings of which are in sight from where you are, and directly on your right is a gateway and cattle grid. If, as I suggested in the introduction to this book, you have brought the relevant OS map with you, you will see that the path should, according to that map, go over the cattle grid and through Linfold Farm. However, recently (1991) the path has been diverted. Now cross over the drive and walk across the field. In front of you are trout ponds surrounded by a timber fence. Walk towards it and with the fence on your right, follow it around to go by a two-way sign. At this point you will go over

17

a plank bridge and, still continuing along by the fence, come to a stile set in the trees in front. Go over the stile and follow the direction of the footpath sign on this short section through the woods. Go over the stile at the end of this path and turn right onto a lane.

Going across Linfold Bridge over the river Kird, continue down the lane to pass by on the right a field gate and footpath sign. Shortly after passing under main grid power lines, and with a field gate and footpath sign on the right, turn right. Going through this gate and ignoring another which will be directly on your right, go through the other gate now facing you. This leads out into a large field. A hedge and trees will be on the right. Walk up this field headland and coming to a gateway go through it. There is a two-way sign on the right. Now in this field bear half left, keeping a barn to your right and at about 200 metres distance. Walk to the opposite corner of the field, going through the gate there and at the footpath sign turn right onto a lane.

Walk on down the lane to the A272 road and turn right onto it. A short distance ahead of you is a public telephone kiosk. Walk towards it and only a few metres beyond turn left and cross over the road and into the entranceway to Bulchins Farm. There is a metal footpath sign at this entrance. With the farmhouse building on the right and going by another building on the left, pass it by going over a stile at a field gate. With a fence now on the right walk up the field headland to a line of trees to the front. On reaching them, go over a stile by a field gate and two-way sign and the path continues down through woodland. Going by a two-way sign on the left, the path will come out into a clearing and here to the left are the buildings of Ingrams Farm, whilst to the front is Redlands Farm. Walk towards its buildings and you will find yourself on a metalled track. Just before reaching the farm with a two-way sign on the left, turn right and go through a gateway into a field.

On the left now is a ditch and hedge and on the other side of this field are three other buildings. Continue along by this hedge and you will shortly come to a two-way sign. Here turn left going over the stile, with the buildings of Redlands Farm now on the left, and continue on through this field. Having first a fence, which gives way to a hedge, on the left, go through a field gate and walk on towards another. Go over the stile here at a three-way sign. Turn right onto the entrance track to the last two farms. This will come out onto a road and, turning right onto it, continue on, crossing a road bridge over a stream. Shortly beyond this and opposite a large thatched house, turn left into a signposted farm track. This will shortly lead to a gateway and cattle grid.

Continue on down the farm track and, coming to a three-way sign on the left, turn left into another farm track. This will continue on for some way and coming to a two-way sign, with Lowfold Farm in front, turn right going through a gateway into a field. Keeping the hedge and trees close by on the right, walk along this field headland and, going through a gateway and now on a grassy track, walk towards a very large oak tree. Just before reaching it and ignoring a field gate to the front, turn left at a two-way sign. Going through a wicket gate into a field, walk across this field to a similar gate on the other side. There is a two-way sign here but its fingerboard is pointing in the wrong direction (1991).

Once through this gate and keeping the hedge to your right, getting occasional glimpses of the river Arun, continue on around the headland of this small field. Coming to an obvious gap in the hedge, make towards it and here on the right is a two-way sign. Crossing a bridged stream here, walk up a slight incline where, at the top, turn right. Go through another wicket gate and the path will clearly follow this field headland. On the right the river will be in clear view for a short way. Coming to a line of oak trees on the right, with the buildings of Harsfold Farm in front and Harsfold Manor on the left, the path will make a junction with a broad farm track. At a three-way sign on the right, turn left onto the track which will shortly bring you to Harsfold Farm. Here the track makes a fork—take the left hand branch to go through a wicket gate. With a barn on the right, continue on past the farm buildings and entranceway into the Manor House. The metalled lane will, after some way, make a junction with the A272 road south of Wisborough Green. The church and other buildings of the village will, of course, have been in sight for some time. With a footpath sign on the other side of the A272, cross over. Walk into the road marked as a cul-de-sac. In only a few yards bear left into the path leading up to the church. Go around the building to the porch and walk down the flagstone path leading away from it, at the end of which and down to your left is a heavy wrought iron gate.

If you want to go into the village for refreshment, go through the gate and down the cobblestone pathway. At the bottom of this path, turn right into the village street. The village pond and the other pub will be to the left but continuing on with houses to right and left, the primary school is also on the right. Shortly you will see the sign for *The Cricketers Arms* pub to your front. When you are ready, simply retrace your steps back to the church.

Having got back onto the flagstone path from the iron gate, turn left, then right. On your left will be a hedge, with the church and churchyard on your right. Walk down the churchyard path then, with a hedge in front of you, turn left to go over a stile and with a three-way sign turn right. Over to your left will be the village school, on your right will be a hedge. Continue along the headland of this field to go through a gap in the line of trees in front of you. With the hedge still on the right, continue to a field gate ahead. With a four-way sign on the left go over the stile and turn left onto a broad farm track and bridleway. With the buildings of Champions Farm appearing on the right, the farm track will make a junction with New Pound Lane, turn right onto it.

Walk up the lane and, coming to Moons-Brook Cottage on the left and crossing the stream bridge just ahead, turn left. Go over a stile at a field gate and footpath sign and in only a few paces go over another stile.

Now walk alongside a hedge and house on the right. At the other end of this small field go over a double stile with a plank bridge between and, walking across this field towards Howfold Farm to your front, at the corner of the building go by a three-way sign. With the farm on your right, make for a gate set in a hedge on the other side of the field. Here, at a four-way sign, go through the gate and turn left on to a broad farm track. During wet weather this can be muddy.

Continue along the length of this track and it will make a junction with a firm stone track; walk ahead into it. Shortly, with houses on the left and making a junction with a road, turn right onto it. Just after going under main grid power lines, turn left off the road to go through an old wicket gateway at the footpath sign, into a field and with a hedge on the left. Continue towards a line of trees in front and following these trees turn left at a two-way sign (you will have seen this some way off) into a woodland path. You will shortly come to a footbridge, go over this to a two-way sign on your left. *Note* The true path should carry straight on but remains blocked as a result of fallen trees. You will, however, see that a clear alternative path has been created, going off to the right and down the bank.

This will, in a short way, lead to a field gate at a two-way sign; go through the gate into a field. A hedge will now be close by on your right—continue along the headland to reach and pass through another gate—continue into this next field. The hedge and trees will still be on the right, pass a pond and gate also on the right. Carry on round the headland and it will come to a very substantial pole hunting fence. Turn right here, going over the stile and with a two-way sign walk along this enclosed grassy path. In about 80 metres and coming to a gate set in the hedge on the left at a two-way sign, turn left. Go over this secured gate, turning right in this field. Again with a hedge on the right, walk on down the headland. It will continue for some way and will eventually force you to take a left and then right turn. Once round the latter, there is a timber power pole at this corner.

Walk on to a gate in front of you. With a large house also to the front, turn right onto the road beyond the gate. With a road junction going off to the right, signposted to Down Hurst Farm, walk straight on and with Boxal Bridge only a few metres in front of you, at a gate and footpath sign on your right, turn right off the road. Having gone through the gate, turn left at the sign into a woodland path. This will then wend its delightful way, first across two plank footbridges and then bring you to a two-way sign. The path continues and will at times be following a stream down on the left; in only one place do you need to watch your direction. Another track will go off to the right—keep to the left and shortly beyond this, the path comes out onto a broad track—bear left onto it. In a few paces and with a three-way sign on the left, the track goes over a bridge. Continue on the short distance to have a house to your front and, keeping it on your left, go through the paddock fence. It has a retractable pole. With the house and fence on your left, walk across the paddock and go over the stile on the other side in the fence. You are again on a woodland path.

With a timber fence also on the left you come to a stile—go over it into a cultivated field. The timber fence will still be on your left for a short distance. The path will then go through some oak trees and, seeing a two-way sign ahead, walk to it and turn left onto a farm track which soon becomes a concrete roadway leading to a large farm. Go through the farmyard gates and with Kirdford church in sight, turn right onto the road.

The village is now directly ahead of you. However, keep to the right and look out for Camel House. Set into its boundary wall, just beyond its entrance, is a plaque and the heading of the text is worth the few minutes it takes to read. It is on the theme 'Degradation of Drunkenness!' Cross the road here and pass the village cross (on your left), also worth reading concerning the history of the village. Your car will be in sight ahead of you.

THE TRUNDLE AND WEST DEAN

WALK 4

★

5 miles (8 km)

Maps 1 : 50.000 scale 197. 1 : 25.000 scale SU 81/91

This almost totally open downland walk has some truly splendid 360°
panoramic views reaching across the Solent to the Isle of Wight, with more
immediate, almost bird's eye views, of Chichester and the Cathedral.
Having recovered from the initial shock of the short, steep climb from The
Trundle car park up the north face of the fort, the remainder of the walk is
over the downland tracks of St Roche's Hill, Lavant and Hayes Downs and
on to West Dean. This small, very interesting village is now administered by
West Dean Estates, and was formerly owned by the late world traveller and
philanthropist, Edward James, whose large house is now the world
renowned West Dean College. The house and the nearby Weald and
Downland Open Air Museum at Singleton are well worth separate visits.

To reach The Trundle car park, from where this walk starts, you should
use the landmark of Goodwood Race Course, 3 miles north of Chichester,
which is well signposted. The car park is at the foot of Trundle Hill.
GR(197)879114.

From the car park, the triangle of land between Town Lane and Knight's
Hill, walk across the road to the stile and footpath sign set alongside a fence,
and walk up the hill (you certainly won't run!). The fence, of course, will be
immediately on your left. Having reached the Neolithic fort ramparts (it
wasn't that painful was it?), the track goes through a wide breach and I
suggest that you get onto the top of the left hand rampart to stop there a few
minutes to take in the views. Walk along the rampart and you will see that
the enclosure fence continues down on your left, as are the race course
grandstands and other buildings. Continue still on the rampart and where
the fence ends, walk down the outer face of the rampart. Now, still with the
fence (its new direction of course) on your left, walk to a stile—the footpath
sign was missing in 1991—go over it. The narrow path descends through a
copse where, at the bottom, there is a three-way footpath sign. Turn right
onto a wide climbing track; go through a field gate and the track continues
across Lavant Down. The course of the track is quite clear on the downside.

You will breast the rise of the Down; Chalk Pit Lane car park will be in
view and will be reached by going over a stile at a field gate where, over on
the right, is a three-way footpath sign. Continue across the car park and
Chalk Pit Lane, on the opposite side of which are two tracks—both have
large logs across them. Take the left hand track and almost immediately on
the right will be a large flint-built house. Here, very noticeably, the tracks go
left and right. There is no footpath sign. Take the wide descending left hand
track; you will have a wire fence on the right and the open expanse of Hayes

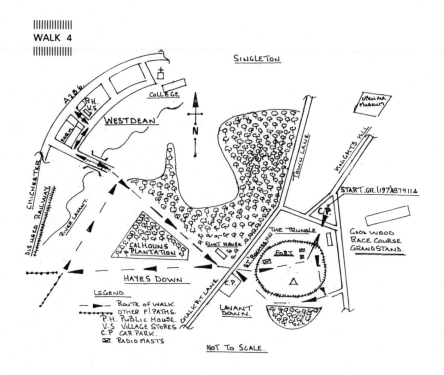

Down on the left. Walk on for some distance to come to a line of trees; go through the gate there, and follow the direction of the two-way footpath sign on your left.

To your front you will see, across the field, the old railway line and a bridge. The downhill track will take you to a gate and three-way footpath sign, turn right. There is now a fence and an occasional hedge on your left. This field path will go through two gates and finally make a junction with a wide stone track running by the flint boundary wall of West Dean Estates. There is a three-way footpath sign here. If you do not wish to continue to West Dean, then simply turn right and follow my directions on returning from the village back to this point. Expecting that you cannot resist the pub or a cream tea, turn left through the gateway and walk down to the bridge over the river Lavant. On the other side, turn right. Walk past the farm on the left and just beyond, with a lovely old house also on the left, turn left into the lane. In only a few yards you will reach the Village Stores on the right, what a pleasant place. *The Trundle Arms* is only a short way further on.

Suitably refreshed, simply re-track your incoming route, back over the bridge and up the ascending track by the boundary wall to the gateway and three-way footpath sign. Continue now, still with the wall on your left, and after some way the track will go through a gateway and there will be woods on either hand.

22

The track continues and will pass on the left, set into the wall, a white painted entrance gate where, shortly beyond, the boundary wall stops. The woodland track continues for another ¼ mile, leaves the trees, and on your left will be the large flint house passed by on the outward leg of this walk.

Cross over now the head of Chalk Pit Lane; continue through the car park area and with the fence on your left go through a gate at the three-way sign, also to the right is the gate you previously came through. The rough stony track, with fences on either hand, will reach on the right a viewing seat . . . what a marvellous place to enjoy the views and sunset of a quiet summer evening. This spot, obviously much loved by John Noon, is dedicated to him and has the legend 'he taught children to love the countryside'.

The Trundle radio masts have been in sight for some time. Shortly beyond John's seat, the track continues across the open floor of the fort. Before leaving, you may want to walk the few yards over to the trig. point from where, at 678 ft (209 m), you have another feast of views, before continuing back on the track. With the twin masts on your left, go through the breach in the fort ramparts (where you came in). Turn left and back down the short hill to the car park.

||||||||||||||||
WALK 5
||||||||||||||||

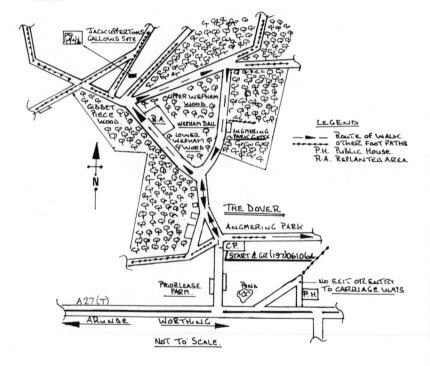

JACK UPPERTONS GALLOWS SITE

UPPER WEPHAM WOOD

GIBBET PIECE WOOD

R.A

WEPHAM DALL

LOWER WEPHAM WOOD

ANGMERING PARK COTTS

LEGEND

— ■ — ROUTE OF WALK
OTHER FOOT PATHS
P.H. PUBLIC HOUSE.
R.A. REPLANTED AREA

N

THE DOVER

ANGMERING PARK

C.P.
START & GR (197)061064

NO EXIT OR ENTRY TO CARRIAGE WAYS

P.H

PRIORLEASE FARM.

POND

A27 (T)

ARUNDE   WORTHING

NOT TO SCALE.

THE DOVER

WALK 5

★

3 miles (4.8 km)

Maps 1 : 50.000 scale 197. 1 : 25.000 scale TQ 00/10

This walk is entirely through woodland over wide footpaths and bridleways. The terrain is very gentle! The woods are an amazing sight in springtime with probably the most prolific display of bluebells hereabouts, so prolific in fact, that their scent is quite heavy. The name 'The Dover' is thought to be a derivation of 'The Dovecot' which was here in medieval times, producing squabs (young pigeons) commercially for the big estates in the district. The walk passes by the site of Jack Upperton's gibbet (gallows), located by a signmarker with the legend as shown in the sketch map. It was on or near this spot that Jack Upperton, in company with an unknown accomplice, held up the local mail carrier, relieving him of money and the mail. For this crime Jack Upperton's body was hung in chains and irons, made by the blacksmith at Burpham for £5. My research shows the execution as having taken place in 1771 whilst the signmarker has it as 1774.

The junction of 'The Dover' lane with the A27 is about 3 miles east of Arundel and 7 miles west of Worthing. The lane is signposted 'The Dover'. Having turned into the lane, proceed up it and you will be directed by notices into 'The Angmering Park Estates' car park, from where this walk starts, at GR(197)061064.

Walk back out of the car park to the lane and turn right to go through a gateway. A footpath sign is on the left. Follow its direction straight ahead to leave the metalled lane with turnings to left and right. Walk onto a stone surfaced track and directly ahead will be a two-way footpath sign—follow its direction. Across the open pasture to the left will be a very handsome flint and brick house and with another two-way footpath sign here on the left, turn right.

This continuing lane, passing a pumping station on the left, will reach (on the left) a pole fence and pole across the entrance into Wepham Woods at a four-way footpath sign. Turn left, immediately now in front the wide track goes up a short incline and levelling off it will pass on the right a large area, reminiscent of a war grave cemetery of white plastic tree protectors to keep deer at bay from the young trees inside. Not far beyond this, the track will reach a gateway and five-way footpath and bridleway sign and here you turn right onto the wide bridleway track.

However, at this point, and with a short section of pole fencing now on the left in which there is a wide gap, you may care to pay your respects to Jack Upperton's marker post! Only just beyond the fence gap walk over to an Angmering Park Estates notice board and stop. Now, with it on your right, the marker (a steel pole set into the ground with the marker notice) will be on your left in the trees, only about 50 ft away. This spot as directed by the Judge 'would be on or as near to the place where the crime was committed' and was where Jack's body hung for two years in its chains and irons. There's no local talk of chains rattling and clanking, so you may proceed in peace once back on the bridleway—(check behind you, just in case!).

Return back onto the intended route, ie the north-bound bridle track, which after some way will pass by on the left a two-way public bridle sign and a fire-fighting open water tank, contained by a fence. Shortly beyond it comes to an offset junction of four crossways. On the far side of this is a four-way sign—turn right. This new, gentle descending track will, after some distance, go through a gateway shortly before passing on the left the large, multi-buttressed building of Angmering Park Cottages, and where in only a few hundred yards you come to the entrance into Wepham Woods on the right.

All that remains now is to retrace your steps back to your motor car.

WEST STOKE AND KINGLEY VALE

WALK 6

★

4.75 miles (7.6 km)

Maps 1 : 50.000 scale 197. 1 : 25.000 scale SU 80/90 and SU 81/91

Arguably the most dramatically beautiful place in Sussex, it will no doubt draw you back time and again and will never fail to delight you with all its changing moods and colours. As soon as you enter the reserve area, you will be aware that I have used nature trail signposts as landmarks but you will also be aware that you will be going in reverse to their direction arrows— why? because you are taking a different, circular, route which is less strenuous and has much better views. I must thank the conservancy wardens for making my task that much easier.

This area contains what is claimed to be the largest yew forest in Europe and when you see its full extent from the Tansley Stone vantage point, I'm sure you will appreciate that claim. The views from the top of The Devil's Humps, the burial mounds of pre-history kings, hence Kingley Vale, at an elevation of 678 ft (206 m), are superb. The area, of course, is a haven for wild life and you will be interested to see on the museum notice board, the daily bird count made by the wardens. Orchids and other wild flowers abound. These paths are not strenuous as I'm sure you will agree. Try also to visit the lovely old church at West Stoke, only a short step away from the car park.

This is the one walk mentioned in the introduction of this book which does not meet the criteria of having a pub directly on or near to the route. However, about ½ mile south at East Ashling is the delightful old pub *The Horse and Groom*. But you will be glad that you have taken a picnic with you as you sit and eat it on the downside at the Tansley Stone in company with the wonderful views from there.

To reach West Stoke, we found it more convenient to take the signposted route off the A27 (the old road), to the Roman Palace at Fishbourne. This serves equally well coming from east or west, then going through East Ashling village to West Stoke. Whilst from the north the A286 road gives good access to turn off at mid Lavant, leading directly to West Stoke and its large car park, from where this walk starts at GR(197)825087.

In the car park, face west and to the left of front will be the Old Rectory. Walk out on to the lane and turn right, and soon the lane bends left at a field gate and stile (you return here). Continue along the lane. Pass Salmon House and Hollandsfield Lodge, both on the right, and beyond and on the left you will pass by the beautiful establishment of Woodend with its mighty Californian Redwood in the grounds. Continuing by the red brick building of Woodend on the left, go by on the right the entranceway to Bowhill

27

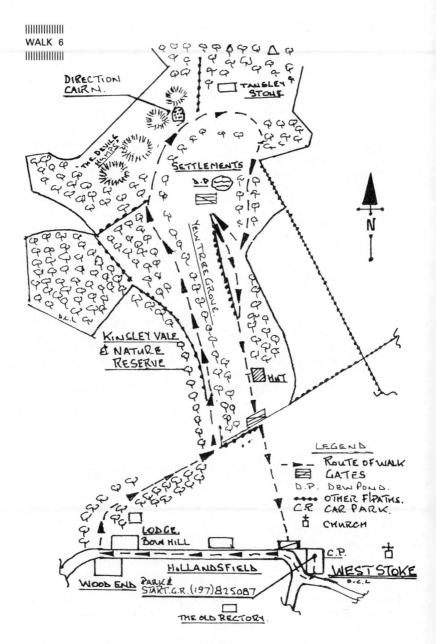

DIRECTION CAIRN.

TANGLEY STONE

THE DEVIL'S HUMPS

SETTLEMENTS

D.P

YEW TREE GROVE.

D.C.L

KINGLEY VALE & NATURE RESERVE

HUT

N

LEGEND
ROUTE OF WALK
GATES
D.P. DEW POND.
OTHER F/PATHS.
C.P. CAR PARK.
CHURCH

LODGE.
BOW HILL

C.P.

WEST STOKE
D.C.L

HOLLANDSFIELD

WOOD END
PARK & START. G.R.(197)825087

THE OLD RECTORY.

NOT TO SCALE.

28

House, where just beyond at a public bridleway sign turn right into a wide track.

At first passing by buildings on the right, this track continues to climb, with woods on either side, before coming out into open ground. Now there are wire fences on either hand. Kingley Vale and Bowhill will be in full view. The fenced path will then come to a three-way footpath sign on the left and here, turn left. There is a Nature Reserve notice here.

This path, also a bridleway, will climb and has bushes on either hand. Very soon and close by on the right on the other side of the hedge you will see the track of another path, also a stile; walk on a short way and through the thinning hedge you will be able to join the path on your right. Having done so, the stile will be behind you and here on the right of the path is a green nature trail post—number 24. Continue up this path with yew trees on either side. Going by post number 23 on your right, come to an area of various other paths. Ignore the one which goes off to your right and walk into the obvious continuation of the path you have just used. Here there will be three other paths to the left of the one you are on.

Continuing now still with yews on either side, pass on the left another green marker post, this time having arrows on it. Coming to a converging track, bear right, passing post number 21 on the right. Here down on your right is the sheer western face of Kingley Vale with hundreds of yew trees— a lovely sight. Pass post number 20 on the right and shortly beyond on the same side number 19, then a marker post with arrows. The track now emerges onto open ground. Here on your left are the four Devil's Humps, the pre-history burial mounds. All four are roughly in line and counting from the end where you are as being the fourth, climb up onto the third, which is the highest, and gaining those extra feet enjoy the views . . . and what views they are, including those of the Isle of Wight. We suggest that you now walk over to the two smaller mounds, where between the two is a flint cairn on top of which is an engraved plate locating various distant landmarks.

To continue the walk and with the cairn at your back, walk down to go over a broad track, on the other side of which you will see a clear downland turf path. Go down its short length and coming to another grassy track, turn left onto it. Here, also on your left, is post number 17. Just beyond is a very clear division of tracks, take the right hand one. Continue to post number 16 also on the right and from here looking up to your left is the large boulder (the Tansley Stone) with its plaque to the memory of Sir Arthur George Tansley, FRS, who secured the future of this wonderful place for the Conservancy Council and the Nation.

Rejoin the path and continue in the same direction as before to pass number 15 post on the left. Shortly beyond go over a stile set in a wire fence, the path still going over the downside of Bowhill. Pass post number 14 on the left and come to a stile on the right set in a fence, at which is a trail post with direction arrows. Go over the stile to enter the yew forest, which will become very dense.

At another trail direction post on your left, bear to the right, then on the right will be post number 13. Bear right. Visible to your left at this point is a wire boundary fence, ignore this path; still continuing through the yew thickets, come to post 12. Turn left and with a wire fence to the right, turn right at the corner, with a marker post. Go over a stile, then at a wide crossing track, turn right onto it.

Coming shortly to a field gate on your right with another close by and facing you, with marker post number 10, turn around and with the gate and post at your back, walk into the obvious gap now facing you between the yews. You are now entering the area containing the largest and oldest trees, many hundreds of years old, whose contorted limbs, twisted and loaded down with the years are, nevertheless, alive and well. The path, very obvious, passes post number 8 on the left, coming then to post number 7. The path comes out onto a grassy track where on your right will be a post bearing numbers 7, 8, 9 (remember that you are walking in reverse direction and not from the museum hut). Turn right. Only a few yards further on and coming to a fork in the paths, take the left hand branch. Coming then to post 6 on the left, bear left, to once again enter this last section of the yew forest.

At post 5, bear to the right, passing between two old yew trees. Here is a notice explaining the area. Coming out by post 4 on the right, turn left, now to be back onto the wide track. Passing post 3 on the left and another on the right, with direction arrows, bear left. Shortly beyond post number 2 is the Conservancy Trust museum hut and there you may be able to purchase literature explaining the background and history of this fascinating place and, of course, you will be able to compare notes with the wildlife daily count notice board.

To return to West Stoke car park, simply go over the stile at the gate by the four-way footpath sign and continue back on this track to it—about ½ mile.

WASHINGTON

WALK 7

★

6 miles (9.6 km)

Maps 1 : 50.000 scale 198. 1 : 25.000 scale TQ 01/11

Washington, the starting location of this walk, is, since the advent of its bypass by the A24(T), a quiet and peaceful place, a charming old village. From your parking place opposite the village pub, the walk goes a very short way on the old road, passing the village post office and store. The next landmark is St Mary's church. Having reached Rowdell and Home Farm Cottages, the track then climbs for about ¾ mile to join the South Downs Way, a long but not particularly steep track and the only climb on this walk. The views are wonderful, extending on a good day to the Isle of Wight. From the South Downs Way there is a very pleasant path down to the Chantry and its ponds, going then across to Sullington, a magical place. Washington, of course, has very easy access by road from every direction and the starting point, the extensive road layby opposite the *Frankland Arms* pub can be reached by turning off the A283 (Steyning to Storrington road) just east of the Washington A24(T) roundabout. GR(198)122129.

At the public layby opposite the pub, face south, ie the pub is on your right, and walking on the pavement continue up to The Street and turn right into it. Keeping to the pavement on the right, passing the post office and village store and St Mary's church, go across the roadbridge over the A24(T). There will be a three-way bridleway and footpath sign on the other side and on the left. Walk on down this metalled lane coming shortly to a fork. Take the right hand branch; there is a two-way sign here. The buildings to the front approaching the fork are Home Farm Cottages; the right hand fork will take you towards the buildings of Rowdell. Coming to a three-way sign, turn left to go down a short section of grassy path and, going through a wicket gate at another three-way sign, walk ahead onto a broad farm track. A stone-built house will be on the right. Pass shortly on the left a red tiled and white panelled house—Home Farm Cottages.
    This broad track will continue to climb until it meets and is signposted with the South Downs Way, and you will turn right onto the Way. Once you are on the Way, continue through a gateway and across a cattle grid. There will be another gate on your left with a track going down to Cobden Farm, a two-way South Downs Way sign will also be on the right here.
    Walk on across the open downland path. Soon a large open-fronted barn will appear, this building has been a good friend to us (and many others) in times past during bad weather. Continue towards it, then 100 metres or so before reaching it, turn right going through a gateway at a three-way sign, also on the right.
    Continue on the broad chalk track going down Sullington Hill, which

31

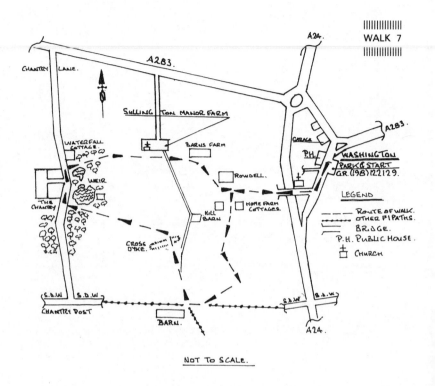

NOT TO SCALE.

soon goes through a gateway and over a cattle grid, whilst on the left you will pass a three-way sign. Above you to the front on the downside by a fence will be another footpath sign, but for a short way keep to the chalk track. Then with a three-way sign on the left and slightly above you, go up to it and turn right. Now you are on a broad grassy track—and if you wonder why did I not direct you here in the first place from the two preceding signs, I simply think it is easier!

Directly in front of you now will be some large grassed earth mounds—an ancient dyke fortification, and the path quite clearly continues through them. You will, of course, now be above the chalk track which you see leading to Hill Barn away to your right. Coming then to a three-way bridleway sign you will bear left, and Sullington Manor Farm and church will be to your right. This path, which is now sunken, will continue downhill. You will have trees to the front and through them the buildings of Chantry.

Going through a field gate the path continues its sunken way, bearing to the right, with the Chantry mill and weir ponds in sight. The path will go through a gate into the woods and shortly you will come out onto Chantry Lane, turn right onto it. Now on the left you will pass by the buildings on the old medieval site of the mill and priory, whilst on the right are the ponds that supplied the power to it. In your own good time you will continue on past this beautiful place, still on the lane, to reach the waterfall and cottage of that name on the right. Here on the right, at a bridleway sign, turn right to go through a field gate, then another with a two-way bridleway sign. Waterfall Cottage of course is on the left. This, sometimes muddy, track will climb up through woods coming out onto open ground. With a fence on the left walk on towards the buildings in front of you, Sullington Manor Farm and the church. In the church, for a few pence, you can obtain a booklet, *Yesterday in Sullington* by R.L. Hayward, whose quote sums up this extraordinarily beautiful place:

'A thousand years in thy sight are but as yesterday when it is past'

The booklet goes on to describe farm and church, all of which makes fascinating reading.

Leaving the church by its eastern gate and opposite the lychgate, turn right and with barns on the right, turn left through a gateway at a two-way bridleway sign into a field. With a hedge on the left continue round this field headland and, coming to a gateway at another bridleway sign, go through it, then another. Now the path is enclosed by hedge and fence and, coming to a three-way sign on the left, bear right. Shortly the path passes between buildings, with Barns Farm upon the left.

The path, soon to become a broad track, continues through a field gate with a two-way bridle sign. Having passed by the paddocks of Barns Farm on the left you will soon have Barns Farm Cottages and the buildings of Rowdell to your front. On reaching the first stone-built house on the right you should now recognise where you are. Just beyond this house at the three-way sign, turn left through the wicket gate, going up the short grassy track. Turn right at the top at the three-way sign to walk down the lane and turn left at the fork. This is where I leave you to walk back across the bridge and through the village to your starting point.

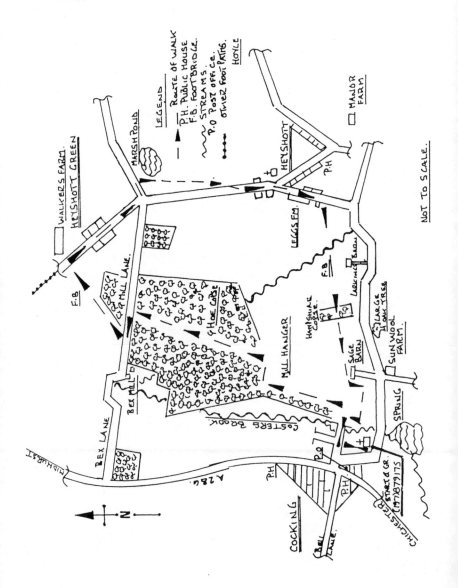

COCKING, HEYSHOTT GREEN AND HEYSHOTT

WALK 8

★

4 miles (6.4 km)

Maps 1 : 50.000 scale 197. 1 : 25.000 scale SU 81/91

The old village of Cocking, dissected by the busy A286 road, manages quite successfully to hide some very pleasant surprises for you. Hopefully you will have your camera with you. A famous personality of this area, Heyshott in particular, was Richard Cobden MP, 1804–1865. His considerable reforming achievements are too numerous to quote here but if, as I hope, you visit the church at Heyshott, you can pay your respects to this man. He had a pew in this church which is still *in situ*, and there is also a memorial plaque to him.

Despite its proximity to the towering downs, this interesting and varied walk through farm, woodland and villages is over gently undulating countryside, but we should warn you that the footpath going north from Mill Lane becomes a stream bed after periods of rain and you will need to be well shod—call it an 'adventure path'!

Cocking lies north of Chichester and south of Midhurst on the A286 road. The walk starts at Cocking church. To reach it, turn off the A286 at Cocking into Mill Lane, on the corner of which is the village post office and general stores, next door to a garage (turning right if coming from Chichester, turning left of course if coming from the Midhurst direction). Once into the junction of Mill Lane, turn immediately right. Now at the back of the post office, continue down this *single track lane* to reach, in a few hundred metres, the church and war memorial. Here restricted parking is available, and you will see that other lane-side verges also have the same facility for parking but *please* make sure that you tuck your vehicle well out of the way of the constant farm traffic here. GR(197)8/9175.

Assuming that you have secured a parking place at the war memorial, walk into the churchyard through the iron kissing gate, taking the path to the big iron gate at the other end past the church, which is certainly worth calling at. Once through the gate you will be in the lane and going by the buildings of Manor Farm on the left. Walk on to the junction with Mill Lane and with a white signpost on the corner, turn right to go over the bridge between the mill feeder pond and the race way, the channel of water constricted to supply the force to turn the old mill wheel during its working life. Sadly only the buildings remain.

Continue on past the race—to have a gateway directly in front of you. Over to your right by other buildings will be a footpath sign. It will direct you into a restricted footpath which will climb up and reach a three-way footpath sign on your right. Walk straight on into a copse—the mill stream will be below and on your left. Coming out of the woods, now with them on your left and a large field on your right, the path continues around the headland of this field, coming to a two-way footpath sign at a ruined gateway. Turn left, going down a short steep bank, in a few yards turning right at a two-way footpath sign. The footpath continues on a wide grass track to another two-way sign. Here, turn left—woods are to the left.

Coming next to a crossing track, continue straight ahead into woods with a two-way footpath sign on the left. Immediately beyond and reaching a fork in the track, continue into the right hand branch. Coming out of the wood at a two-way footpath sign, walk on to another wood to your front, with conifer nurseries left and right. Coming then to a two-way footpath sign, turn right, shortly reaching a T junction of tracks, and with a two-way footpath sign on the left, turn left.

This track is now on easy going, firm, dry stone. Passing on the right one other footpath sign, it will continue to a gate. Go through this and turn left onto Bex Lane. Walk on for about 100 metres, coming to a single-way footpath sign on your right, and turn right into a woodland path.

This is the path mentioned in the introduction to this walk and is liable to be wet, but no problem at all if you have good footwear. Coming to the footbridge at the end of this path, cross it and turn immediately right to have to your front a green painted steel gate with a stile and three-way footpath sign. Cross over the stile into a grassy track and continue to a field wicket gate at a two-way footpath sign. Go through this gate into a small field, on the other side of which are the houses of Heyshott Green to the right, with stables and farm buildings on the left.

Walk towards the stables and on the right of this building go over a stile. Bearing to your right around cottages, walk onto a tarmac surfaced lane. Continue on the short distance to a crossroad where you will see directly in front of you the church and other buildings of Heyshott village. A simple matter to walk the few hundred yards down the road to the village, but there is the alternative to walk on a footpath across the greensward. To do so turn left at the crossroad and in about 30 metres, turn right at a timber footpath sign (not the metal one a little further on). Once on this path, Marsh Pond will now be on your left. Continue down the length of this greensward and, coming to a footpath sign, you will come back onto the road and will have the houses of the village on either hand. In only a few metres reach the church of St James.

If you would like to spend some time in the church and refresh yourself at the pub, turn left into the churchyard through an iron gate and eventually leave through another at the end of the path (wasn't that a lovely old church—and did you see Richard Cobden's pew?). Once out of this gate, turn left to walk on the short distance to the *Unicorn* pub. On your return, walk back to the church.

Walk on to the road junction; with a telephone kiosk to your front, turn left and walk by the Richard Cobden Club hall on the left. Continue on by the farm and other buildings to reach an old house, The Old Thatch. Walk on beyond it and its chained off area of grass, where just beyond and on your right there is a green painted steel gate with a two-way footpath sign (damaged). Go over the stile into a field. Once in this field and going up its rising ground, you will see the next footpath sign ahead of you. Go over the stile here into another field where now on your right will be a hedge and a line of oak trees.

Next go over a stile and footbridge. Larkings Barn is to your left across the field, with Hampshire Copse in front of you. Continuing down the field the hedge will end. Go over a plank footbridge and the path across this field enters Hampshire Copse through a ruined gate, at which is a two-way footpath sign (damaged). The short path through the copse will come out into a cultivated field. Over to your left, quite close by, is a hedge which, further along its length, has an obvious corner. Walk towards it to another two-way footpath sign (also damaged in 1991, but the last one). Now over on your left will be a very large oak tree. Reaching the top of the rise in this field there will be in very clear view across the field a gap in the hedge—walk through it across a farm track and through the opposite gap to go straight across this cultivated field on a wide path. You will now see your last landmark on this walk—Sage Barn. At the footpath sign at the back of this building, turn left, then right at the hedgerow, which you will follow down to an opposing hedge and turn right. You will have seen a two-way footpath sign and on reaching it, turn left. At the bottom of the bank, in which steps have been cut, is a three-way footpath sign, which you passed by on the outward leg of this walk—turn left.

From this point, you will simply retrace your steps back to the church and your car. Before doing so you will doubtless pause a while. If the race is in spate, the water pouring down it and over the two weirs is a pretty sight and you get a better view of it going this way.

MIDHURST

WALK 9

★

9.5 miles (15.2 km)

Maps 1 : 50.000 scale 197. 1 : 25.000 scale SU 81/91 and SU 82/92

According to the *History of Sussex* written by Mark Lower in 1870, Midhurst—'Although not rich in historical associations, possesses much picturesque beauty and a most salubrious climate.' (What delightful phraseology). Starting from this pleasant country town you will soon be among its farms. In fact, the outward path goes through the stable yards of one farm, then wanders across farmland and crosses the A272. You will be delighted with the deeply sunken path which then takes you through another farm and on to Lodsworth—a lovely old village. St Peter's, set in its arboretum-standard churchyard, contains among all the other fine specimens, the largest Peruvian Pine (Monkey Puzzle tree) that I know of. The walk takes you past the old pub and continues over downland with good views. It continues through woods and finally goes down the delightful sweet chestnut-lined avenue called The Race and back to Midhurst via the polo grounds.

The town of Midhurst is readily accessible via the cross country A272 or north to south A286 roads. The walk starts from the large town centre car park (free) which is also the bus arrival and departure point: the location is at GR(197)887218. I find it very convenient to park at the east end of the car park (opposite end to the toilet block).

From there go through the wicket gate to the left and turning right, walk down to Cowdray House ruins. Turn right just before the bridge over the river Rother. With the river on your left, and shortly going through a wicket gate, continue along the bank path. Ignore a track going off to the right and keep to the bank path—it will come to an area containing a water pumping station and industrial buildings. At the three-way sign, turn left and walk across the tarmac to a (canal) bridge opposite. Go over it and shortly beyond there will be a cottage on the left with a stile and three-way sign in front. Turn left into a beautiful woodland path which will give you a good view of the Cowdray House ruins, which you will look down onto across the river. Coming to a two-way sign on the right, go through a gate and, with Balls Barn Farm now in front, walk on to the gates. The path continues into the stable yards where, just beyond and with a two-way sign on the right, walk on down the metalled lane.

With a stone-built house on the right and footpath sign on the left, the lane crosses into Selhurst Road. Walk into the road. Straight ahead a footpath sign is on the right. The road goes up a short incline here. It will continue for some way to pass by Great and Little Todham Farms on the left, between and on the right a footpath sign at some estate houses. Passing

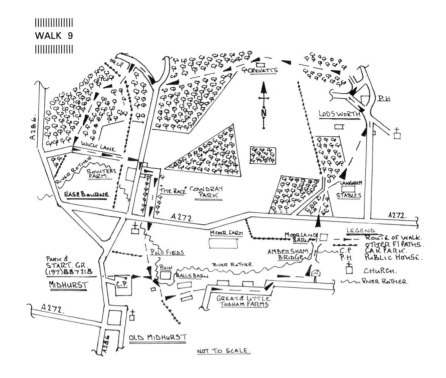

the last of the Little Todham buildings on the left, continue for about 300 metres and at a bend in the road turn left, then right. This goes off the road and through a wide gap in the hedge into a field. A footpath sign is on the right. With a hedge on the right, walk along this headland to a large oak tree in front. On reaching it, there is a two-way sign. Turn left and walk on the path in the centre of this field. Coming then to a two-way sign, it will direct you to another a short way ahead; the buildings of Moor Farm are to your left. With trees and the river below, also on the left, with fields on the right, the headland will come to a stile and two-way sign. Turn left over the stile to go down a bank into a water meadow. Endeavour to keep near to trees on the left. Then Ambersham Bridge will come into view. Go through the gate there, at a footpath sign. Turn left and go over the bridge, passing the entrance to Moor Farm on your left—go by a house on the left then Moorland Barn on the right.

This lane will continue and will be flanked by high sand embankments. It will then come to the A272 road and, with the road direction signs, walk into the path opposite. There will be a footpath sign on the right. This delightful sunken path will all too soon come out onto a lane at a ruined gateway. On the right is a two-way sign. Turn immediately right through a gate and on either side of you are the buildings of Gosdensheath Farm. Walk across the field to have the building with its hedge nearest you on your left and this will put you onto a broad sandy track. Follow the hedge around on your left and coming to a wood you will come to a gateway. The sandy track carries on through this gate, going up an incline to another gate on the other side of the lane, with a two-way sign here. Go through the gate and, coming to a large oak tree on your right and power line pole on the left, turn left to go over the stile at a two-way sign into a cultivated field.

With trees and hedge on the left, continue around this headland to pass two more footpath signs. Langham's Stables will now be in view. Then, coming to a third two-way sign, turn left and, going through the trees, come out into an open field. Now, bearing slightly right, walk to a fence across the field. Lodsworth House and the village buildings are now in clear view. You will then see a stile set in the fence. Go over it and walking to another fence, go over this stile also. Keeping the hedge and fence on your right the headland will come to another stile in a fence. Shortly beyond this, go over this last stile at a footpath sign. Go down some stone steps, turning left onto the village lane and walk on. You will come to a junction going off to the right. There is a half-timbered house here: The Old Nursery.

It would be a pity to miss a visit to the old church and its collection of beautiful specimen trees—to do so you simply turn right at the junction. The church is only a few minutes away and when you are ready, return to this junction and turn right, continuing up through the village. This brings you to *The Hollist Arms* pub. Turn left, there is a telephone kiosk on the left and on the green outside the pub is a three-way timber sign. Your way is directed to The Sports Field.

Continue on up the lane with houses on the right and, opposite a large pair of wrought iron gates on the left, turn right with The Croft on the right. Bear left to go past on your left the entranceway into Oakfield, numbers 1–10, then a little further on Oakfield numbers 11–23. Still bearing left, with Beechfield and a footpath sign on the left, turn left off the lane into a wide stony track, and passing by a bungalow, Vining, continue still on this track. The surface character will not change for some time and it is a good direction guide to ignore other tracks which will go off to left and right. Climbing gently, the path continues with woods on either hand and a large area of coppiced chestnuts. Ahead a power pylon will come into view. Go through an old gateway; on the right is a three-way sign and to your left you will see Vinings Farm. Turn right to go through another gateway. The grid pylon is now in front of you. Passing a four-way sign on the left and with the pylon now on the right, go through another gateway. The buildings of Grevatts Farm will be ahead whilst on the right is a deep valley.

You will come first to a reservoir and Grevatts Farm, both on the left, and a four-way sign on the same side. Turn left to go through a gate into the farm. Bear right to go through the gate in front. Now with a fence on the left and a cultivated field on the right, walk towards a gateway ahead with woods beyond. Go through the gate, there is a two-way sign on the right. The woodland track continues straight on. Coming to another two-way sign on the left just beyond a crossing track, and to a fork, continue into the right hand path. Go a short distance downhill and through a gate at the bottom.

There is a footpath sign on the right. The lane you are now on goes to the left, but turn right and walk into the lane junction opposite. At the top of the rise, turn left to go through a gateway at a footpath sign. Continue down this grassy track and, coming to a fork with a footpath sign in front, take the right hand branch. Passing a watch tower on the left, the track will make a junction with another track. With a two-way sign in front, turn left onto the other track. It will continue for some distance and with remnants of old stone walls on either hand. Continue through woods, passing under power lines, and with a two-way sign on the left, turn left into a narrow tree-lined path. This will come to a crossing track. With a three-way sign on the left, turn left into Wick Lane—a reservoir is on the right. Go through a steel gate.

Wick Lane then comes to a crossing lane, with the lane continuing to the right. Walk straight ahead to go up a bank and over the stile at a two-way sign. Now in a field and with buildings in front, walk towards them. The way across the field is determined by a ridged path. Coming to a stile in a fence, go over it and then another into a short track between buildings to turn right onto Easebourne Street. Continue down the street until you come to a footpath sign on the left, the entrance to Love's Farm. Turn left into the next entranceway between a house: 'The Barn' and 'Cullens Yarde'. This is a 'permissive path', not a right of way but available as a footpath with the full permission of the landowner who reserves the right of closure. It continues first by a wall on the right, then between hedge and fence. Then at the top there will be an old ruined wall on the left. Here, turn right into the avenue of The Race; an uninterrupted wide grass track lined for its entire length with old Spanish chestnut trees. It continues its impressive way to finally go through a pole gate onto the A272 road.

Cross the road and continue into the signposted path opposite with the old church and priory on the right. Go through a gateway ahead and the way continues on a sandy stone track. Going by the polo fields on the left you are heading now towards Cowdray House ruins in front of you. Go through gateways, bearing left at a footpath sign and, with iron railings now on the left enclosing the ruins and museum, turn right. Cross the bridge over the river Rother and opposite the ruins simply walk back to the car park now ahead of you.

||||||||||||
WALK 10
||||||||||||

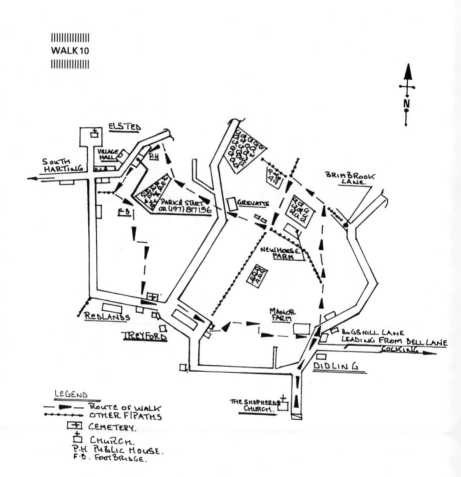

N

ELSTED

SOUTH HARTING

VILLAGE HALL

P.H

PARK & START
OR (197) 817196

F.B

GREVATIS

BRIMBROOK LANE

NEW HOUSE FARM

MANOR FARM

REDLANDS

TREYFORD

BUGSHILL LANE
LEADING FROM BELL LANE
COCKING

DIDLING

THE SHEPHERDS CHURCH.

LEGEND
— ROUTE OF WALK
•••• OTHER F/PATHS
⊞ CEMETERY.
⛪ CHURCH.
P.H PUBLIC HOUSE.
F.B FOOTBRIDGE.

NOT TO SCALE.

ELSTED

WALK 10

★

5 miles (8 km)

Maps 1 : 50.000 scale 197. 1 : 25.000 scale SU 81/91

As with Walk 8, this ramble is dominated by the towering presence of the Downs. With the varying degrees of light and colour change, they can be very beautiful and they supply a wonderful backdrop for this walk. Going through three tiny villages and across undulating farmland, this area is very rural and off-the-beaten-track. Elsted, via South Harting, has good access from the south, west and north, but you will still need to appreciate that it is very rural and its approach lanes were intended for horse traffic. The approach from the east, turning off at Cocking into Bell Lane from the A286, really is something else, and is single track lane for the 3 miles from Cocking to Elsted. Once into Elsted parking is easy, in the *Three Horse Shoes* pub car park where Mr Burdfield, the pub landlord (1991) welcomes you to use his facility. Alternatively, the large parking area of the village hall is opposite. The starting point of this walk, the pub car park, is at GR(197)817196.

In the pub car park, face south, ie with the Downs to your front. Walk on a few paces to turn right and go over a stile at a footpath sign leading into the garden of the house here. There are paving slabs set in the lawn across to a wicket gate leading into an enclosed path. Go over a stile, coming to another at a three-way footpath sign. Once over this stile and now in a field, turn immediately left with a hedge on your left. The descending field path will come to a stile (damaged) and a footbridge—go over it, coming shortly to a two-way footpath sign where there is a stile. Go over it and turn immediately right. With a wire fence on the right, continue to a large oak tree, passing it to reach a fence facing you—turn left. Now with fence and stream on the right, come to another stream with a footbridge between stiles. Continue into the next field, hedge and stream still on your right, to reach a stile and two-way footpath sign at a field gate. Go over the stile and turn right.

    With a hedge and wire fence on the right, walk down this field path towards a house called Treyford Cottage where, on reaching the lane, turn left. Passing a cemetery on the left, come to a lane junction and turn right—signposted Treyford and Cocking. Coming to Rubin Cottage, turn left into the lane junction here. Go by a house on the right, North Garden. Continue on to pass by a footpath sign on the left at a house. At the corner of the lane with a footpath sign on the right, turn left, the wide grassy track going between two houses.

    Going into a copse, the path comes to a stream bridge and stile—go up this short, steep incline and go over another stile at the top. Ignore the two redundant stiles on the right and with trees on the right, walk along this field edge, where in about 500 yards, come to a stile at a two-way footpath sign on the right. Go over the stile and turn left.

Now, with the tree/hedge on the left and the buildings of Manor Farm, Didling, to the front, and the church to the right, walk down this field headland. Coming to a double stile with a two-way footpath sign, go over them to turn left. In a few yards turn right at another two-way footpath sign. Still with the hedge on the left, continue now down this field to reach a bridged stream. Here at a two-way footpath sign is a wire gate operated by an over-centre lever. Be careful as you release its tension and please re-secure it when you have passed through. Turn right and in a few yards, come to a two-way footpath sign and turn left. Going up the rising ground of this field, Manor Farm will be directly in front of you. On reaching a free-standing footpath sign go through (exactly as the previous one) a gate into the farmyard.

Coming out of the farmyard onto the lane, turn right and with tiny St Andrew's church —The Shepherd's Church—in sight, walk down the short distance towards it.

To return to the walk, go back to Manor Farm and with its buildings to right and left, walk on passing Didling Manor and a wall-mounted posting box on the left. Just beyond, turn left at a two-way footpath sign into a broad track. Continue past a house and its garden fence on the left to come out into a field and, with a two-way footpath sign on the left, walk down this field headland, passing a twin power line support. Continue across the open field, coming shortly to a stile and three-way footpath sign on the left. Walk on by them, now with a hedge on the left. Coming to a two-way footpath sign, and going just beyond it, go through another lever-operated gate. Turn right now with hedge fence and stream to the right. Once in this field you will see over to your left, a two-way footpath sign at a steel gate. Walk around the field, go through the gate and, crossing a bridge, go over a stile.

With the bridge, gate and sign behind you, walk now into this field approaching a line of oak trees ahead. There will be a very pronounced gap between two of them. About the middle of the line, between these two oaks, is a bridge over a deep ditch. Going into the next field and with the last bridge behind you, walk on to another line of oaks and in about the same position. Go over a similar bridge and on the opposite side of this field, you will see clearly a stile and footpath sign. Go over this stile and turn left, at the four-way footpath sign, onto the wide grass track of Brimbrook Lane, which has oak trees and ditches on either side.

Now going over another stream with a three-way footpath sign at a bridge, and bearing left into a field, make for a steel field gate on the opposite side. Go through this gate and over another bridge. Walking straight ahead in this field to a line of trees in front, you will pass by on the left a large enclosed brick well head (yes, it's very deep!) and just beyond is a two-way footpath sign. Go over a bridge here and then a stile. On entering this field with a wood and ditch on the left, bear left and walk towards the steel field gate already in sight on the other side of the field.

The buildings of New House Farm will now be in sight on the left, whilst on the right are two farm estate houses. Going through the field gate at a two-way footpath sign, walk across this field towards another gate to your right, ie the gate nearest the two houses. Once through the gate, walk to the farm track and turn right onto it. Continue past the houses on the right and out to the junction with a lane. On your right will be a house, Grevatts. Turn right onto the lane and in only a few steps turn left. Go over a stile at a steel field gate and two-way footpath sign. Walk up the rising ground of this field—in front of you will be a line of trees, aim to pass these on your left. The line of trees makes a right angle and, having the new line of trees now on your left, continue by them.

Shortly to the front and below will be a large oak tree, alongside of which you will see a stile and two-way footpath sign. Go over this stile and the short area of field to cross over another stile and footbridge. Turn left. Some buildings of Elsted are now in view. You will see to your left another two-way footpath sign. Walk the short distance around the field to it and turn left on reaching it to go over a footbridge and stile—turn right. Having done so you will be able to see the next footpath sign in the hedge in front. Walk around the field headland to it. Go through the gap in the hedge and walk into this field, making now for the footpath sign you see on the other side of the field, in front of the village buildings. On reaching the three-way footpath sign, do not go over the stile here, but turn left to have a hedge and timber fence on the right. Walk along the field headland and just where the timber fence ends, turn right through a gap in the fence and walk into the garden of the *Three Horse Shoes* pub.

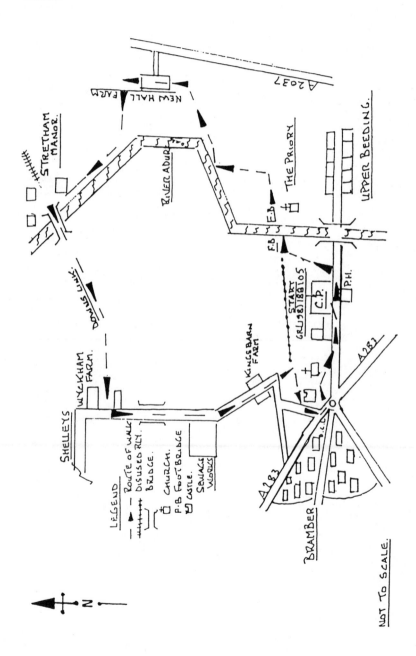

BRAMBER

WALK 11

★

6 miles (9.6 km)

Maps 1 : 50.000 scale 198. 1 : 25.000 scale TQ 01/11 and TQ 21/31

A busy port in Roman and medieval times, little remains now of those eras and as with Washington, since it has acquired a bypass Bramber is a much quieter village. This walk is almost totally flat and its outward leg is across water meadows and through farmland to Streatham Manor, a charming old building. The route back to Bramber is via the Downs Link path, the castle and church. The castle, with sadly only one wall remaining, was started shortly after the Norman Conquest. The remains are owned by the National Trust and the lovely little church, St Nicholas', is well worth a visit.

Access to the village can be from the A24 to the west via the A283 road from Washington, or coming from the east and south, from the A27(T). In either event, there is a large free car park with toilets, which is directly opposite the *Bramber Castle Hotel*. It is from here that the walk starts at GR(198)188105.

Leaving the car park, turn left into the village street and as soon as you are able, cross over onto the pavement on the other side. Walk on and about 50 metres beyond St Mary's House on the right, turn left into a signposted gateway which leads into a field. Bear left across this field and in the corner, with a two-way sign on the left, go across a stream bridge into the next field and follow the farm vehicle tracks across it. Passing a double power line support on the right, continue on towards a two-way sign and go over the bridge there. To your front is the river Adur with a large footbridge over the river. Cross it and once over the stile at the other end (the footpath sign was broken) go down the river bank into the field and walk to its opposite corner—on the right is the priory and church

Very soon, and in front of you, will be your next crossing point. At a two-way sign, go over the stile and you will be on the (south) bank of a wide dyke, which is on your left. Coming to another two-way sign, go over a double stile with a plank bridge between into a large meadow. The path comes to a gate—go through it and in a few paces (and going over a stile at a gate with a three-way sign to your front) turn left onto a broad track going over a bridge at a gate. The wide dyke is again on the left with a blackthorn hedge on the right. Coming to gates on left and right and with a two-way sign on the right, go over a double stile to continue on the dyke bank path. Coming to a bridge, gateway and two-way sign on the left, go over the bridge and bear half right into a water meadow.

Already in sight across this meadow you will see a fence and stile and leading to both is a clear farm vehicle track. Go over both bridge and stile at the fence and again follow the continuing farm tracks. To the front of you on

47

top of the river bank is a three-way sign set in bushes. Once up on the river bank to the three-way sign, another will be to your front. Go over the stile here and bear right, not onto the bank path, nor into the track going through a gate on the right, but walk up the field to a wire fence with a notice on its corner 'Temporary Footpath, please use'. Turning right with the fence now on the left, you will also pass other notices with the same message. There are now some buildings ahead, site cabins and New Horton Farm to the right of them. The notices direct you over a stile in a fence and then over another stile in the opposite fence. The redirected path then rejoins the old, and with a two-way sign on the right, walk towards the ruined buildings of (old) New Horton Farm.

Passing by the buildings the track continues through a gateway. The buildings of New Hall Farm are in front. Once past the gate, turn immediately right and now in front is a three-way sign—walk to it. Turn left here and across the other side of the field you will see quite clearly the side rails of a timber footbridge set in a hedge which is your objective. (Here I must explain that when I walked this route the intervening field had been put down to ridged up potatoes and the fieldpath had not been re-instated. Quite simply I went back on myself about 30 metres, then I turned right to walk down between the potato crop and a wheat crop in the same field which gave me easy access across the field to the other side of it. With the footbridge now well in sight, I turned right then left over the bridge.)

Going over a stile the path is enclosed, and with the buildings of New Hall Farm on left and right, continue into the farm and, coming to a gate, go through it. In front is a two-way sign at a silo, turn right. You are still among the farm buildings and in a few steps and with another two-way sign in front of you, turn left and walk beyond the buildings to a crossing farm track. Turn left again and with a large bungalow in front turn right into the continuing farm track. A large notice proclaims this to be 'Private Access' to New Hall Farm and Streatham Manor—remember my introduction observation on such notices and be assured that you are on a Public Right of Way which, in only a short way ahead is confirmed by a three-way sign, one finger of which (of course) is pointing back down the way from which you have just come.

Turn left here and you will soon be passing by, on the left, New Hall Farm house. Other farm buildings will be over on the right. Walk on down this metalled farm track and then with the entranceways to Streatham Manor and the farm buildings on your right, and bearing left and having a two-way sign on your right, turn right and walk down the field headland. A hedge is on your right. You will very soon come to the river bank path. Turn right over a stile at a two-way sign and join the bank path. To the front is Streatham Manor and the old railway bridge across the river. Go over the stile and turn left to go over the bridge. You are now on the Downs Link Path as the next footpath sign will tell you. The old rail track bed is now stretched out in front of you and along its length you will go across two more old bridges. Coming to a two-way sign on the left, turn right and go up the bank to turn left at the top. With a three-way sign on the right, turn left to go over a stile; ie not continuing on the Downs Link.

Once over the stile and in the field follow the headland down with a hedge and the old line on your left to go through an old gateway. There on your left will be a stile and three-way sign. Now in a water meadow, bear over to your right and, keeping the sparse hedge and fence on the right, continue along and around this headland. With the buildings of Wyckham Farm close by, turn left to walk across the field. Go through the gateway between the farmhouse and the barns, and go through the yard and out of the gateway there. On your right is a three-way sign; turn left—back onto the Downs Link Path. This broad, stony track will continue on for about ¾ mile. Passing a two-way sign and Wyckham Dale Cottages on the left, and next going over a railway bridge, you will note that the Downs Link Path goes right here, whilst you continue on; passing an industrial site and treatment works on the right. You are now in Barns Farm Lane and you will then pass by Kings Barn Farm on the left. Shortly beyond this, and with modern houses in front, pass by the entranceway to Barn Croft on the left and just beyond turn left to go over a stile. The three-way sign was missing here in 1991.

Walk on down this field; there will be a fence on the right. In front is a gate and across the field is the footbridge over the river you walked over on the way out. Now just before reaching the gate, turn right. The three-way sign was also missing here. To the right is a fence with houses beyond and down on the left a dyke. Coming to a stile at a gateway and footpath sign, go over it into a woodland path. Then coming to a fork, take the left hand path and, going between timber power line supports and with a three-way sign on the left, continue straight on. You will pass a two-way sign on the right— the path comes out onto Castle Lane. Turn left on to it and here you must cross the lane and get onto the pavement on the other side.

Going by Castle Cottage on the right and coming then to Bramber village bypass roundabout, cross over to the left hand side of Castle Lane and take the signposted entranceway to the castle and church. Going this way has the added advantage of bypassing a section of village road and is much more pleasant. You can take this opportunity to visit the castle and St Nicholas' church. On leaving, walk back through the lychgate, turning left, and you will shortly be back on Bramber village street to make your way back to the car park.

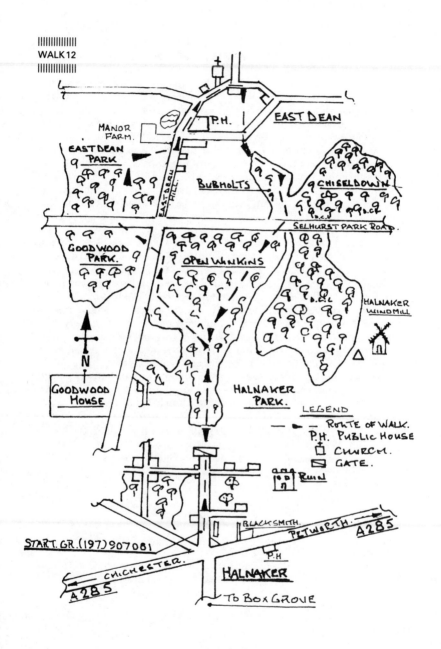

|||||||||||||
WALK 12
|||||||||||||

NOT TO SCALE.

HALNAKER AND EAST DEAN

WALK 12

★

7 miles (11.2 km)

Maps 1 : 50.000 scale 197. 1 : 25.000 scale SU 80/90 and SU 81/91

This delightful walk goes at first through Halnaker Park with its ancient Spanish chestnuts and the remains of the priory, gently climbs up to Goodwood Country Park, and descends then through the woods of East Dean Park and down into the village of East Dean. Here the route goes past the village pub and on up to the church. You will climb up into Bubholts Woods and, on reaching the Selhurst Park road, the way back is then all downhill through the woods of Open and Lady Winkins (a Saxon enclosure). Although in the midst of the Downs it is not a strenuous walk and the views are magnificent.

Halnaker crossroads, from where this walk starts, lies on the A285, Chichester to Petworth road, 3 miles north of Chichester from the A27(T). Having reached the crossroads and with the junction to Boxgrove on the right, turn left into the entranceway to Halnaker House (not signposted)—do not mistake the road also turning left but which is signposted to Goodwood. Once into the entranceway there is adequate verge parking on the left by Goodwood Park boundary wall. A row of houses is on the right, on the other side of a hedge, and please ensure you are tucked out of the way of farm traffic. This is the start of the walk at GR(197)907081, with the sketch map being explicit on this location.

Leaving your motor car, face north, with the houses on your right and boundary wall on the left. Walk up this track to pass by Park Cottage on the left. Going over a cattle grid you are now in Halnaker Park with its ancient Spanish chestnut trees and the priory ruins. Coming then to the buildings of Little Halnaker on the right and the massive gate pillars in the boundary wall, walk ahead to go through a field gate; there is a two-way footpath sign on the left.

With the park boundary wall still on your left, walk the length of this field to go through another gate and now continue on a bridleway with woods on either hand. *Note* after rain, this track—especially at this point near the gate—can be very muddy and churned up by horses. You do, however, have the alternative just past the gate of diverting into a secondary path on the left created by other walkers. Its course is quite clear. Returning as you must to the bridleway you will, after some time, go through a gateway. Just beyond, with a three-way footpath sign in front, turn left into the footpath.

This climbing chalk and stone farm track will come to open ground on the left, with woods still on the right. Across this open ground are views to the coastal plain and Chichester harbour. Levelling out, the track will have thicket woods on either hand, and it will bend round to the left on coming to a large open field. Ahead you will see a two-way footpath sign. On reaching it, but not going by it on to the lane, turn right. The path now continues on the field headland; a hedge is on the left, on the other side of which is the lane.

To the right now are downland views and quite close on its hill is Halnaker windmill, a splendid landmark. The headland path continues to a two-way footpath sign. Turn left past a ruined stile onto the lane and turn right. In only a few feet turn left off the lane into the entrance to a field through a gateway, at a footpath sign. Across this short section of field you will see a stile and a two-way footpath sign. Go across the field, going over the stile to continue on a woodland path. It will reach a timber fence and two-way footpath sign. Going through a gap in the fence you are now in the parkland of Goodwood Country Park. With trees and picnic benches to the front, walk through the trees to a toilet block which is now in sight to the front. Keeping this to the left, go through the gate to the right, and just beyond the toilet, go through the gateway. On the right is a two-way footpath sign. Go across the road (Selhurst Park Road) and walk into the track opposite.

Ignoring tracks going off to right and left (there is a three-way footpath sign at the left one) continue straight ahead and you will go by a single-way footpath sign now on the left.

This unmistakable wide farm track will continue on for some way, coming eventually to a gate. Go through this gate, there are the remains of a footpath sign here. Coming out now into an open grass area there are trees close at hand on the right. Keeping these trees close by and walking by those that will jut out into the field, continue on. Trees will also be close by on your left, and the field is terminated by trees in front of you—the village of East Dean will now appear through these trees.

Now bear to your left and go through a very obvious gap in the trees. The path which now starts to descend comes to a gate. Go through it, walking down this field making for a corner formed by a hedge on the right. All the buildings of Manor Farm and East Dean are now before you. With a grid pylon on the left you will now have a two-way footpath sign in front. On reaching it turn right. This path will at first have wire fences on either hand, then with a fence only on the left it will continue across these fields coming to a gateway leading onto a lane, East Dean Hill, with a footpath sign on the right. Turn left onto the lane.

Passing by the entrance to Manor Farm on the left, continue on into the village. The green and pond will be on the left and with *The Hurdle Makers* pub now in sight continue on towards it. The walk continues beyond the pub and you will find it safer here to cross over to the pavement on the other side of the road, passing the village hall on the left, then The Old Vicarage on the right. Turn off left into the signposted path up to the church. This lovely old building, very simple and uncluttered, is the resting place of 'William Peachey, Blacksmith, Swordmaker to Oliver Cromwell and his officers', who died in 1688. William's memorial stone is set into the east facing wall of the church just around to the right of the porchway; hard to imagine that this man's fame as a craftsman had reached out from this tiny rural place to the Roundheads looking for the best in weapons of that time.

Returning back to the road, turn left, passing Droke Farm on the right, then going by a post box in a house wall on the right. Just beyond the house, turn right into a signposted footpath which leads now across the village sports field. Walk towards a pair of animal drinking troughs and just beyond at a footpath sign, go over a stile to turn left onto the path. In a few yards turn right to go through a gateway (there is a footpath sign missing here). The path climbs up this field and with fence and then trees on the right, towards the gate leading into the distinctive heart-shape of Bubholts Wood; this gate will have been in sight for some time. Go through it and a few paces beyond, turn left at a three-way sign on the right.

This delightful path continues uninterrupted for some way. It will bend to the right and shortly beyond, bend left, then come to a two-way footpath sign. Go over the stile here, coming out immediately into a field. Walking across it come to another two-way footpath sign. Go over this stile and the path continues through Bubholts Woods.

Reaching a crossing track with a four-way sign on the left, turn left. Directly in front of you now and at the end of this broad track, is a field gate. However in about 20 paces from the four-way sign, turn right off the track into a path which will shortly come out onto an open field, on the other side of which you will see a footpath sign. Walk across the field and go over the stile, crossing over the road (Selhurst Park Road). Walk into a wide woodland track; a two-way footpath sign is on the right. Continuing straight on, you will walk on beyond a large solitary beech tree on the right, and then, approaching a gate, turn right before going throught it. There will be a two-way footpath sign now in the trees on your left.

You are now at the top of the long descending path (about a mile through the woods of Lady and Open Winkins and from here you will see almost the whole of its length. Before descending down into the woods, the view again reaches across the coastal plain to Chichester, the cathedral and beyond.

Eventually the Winkins track goes through a pole gateway and just beyond on the right is a three-way sign, which you will, no doubt, recognise as having turned left at on the outward leg of this walk.

Now go straight ahead and going through the gateway which will also be familiar, continue on this bridleway through the woods. (Don't forget that you can avoid the muddy sections by diverting to your right, taking the secondary path in the trees). Go then through the open parkland to reach your car at the end of the lane at Halnaker.

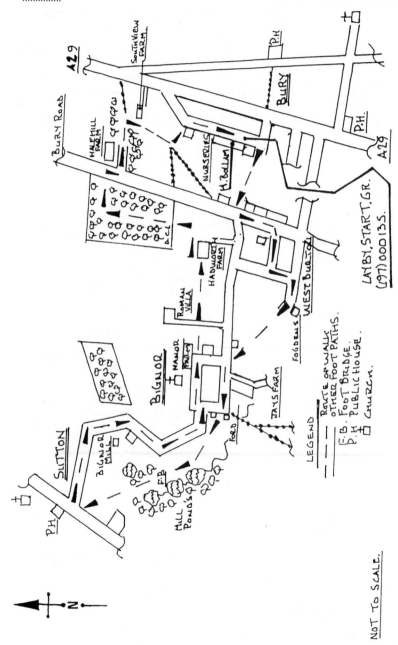

NOT TO SCALE.

BURY AND BIGNOR ROMAN VILLA

WALK 13

★

5 miles (8 km)

Maps 1 : 50.000 scale 197. 1 : 25.000 scale SU 01/11 and SU 81/91

A walk in the shadow of the Downs at the foot of West Burton and Bury Hills, with the attraction of being able to visit the Roman villa at Bignor. The returning footpath goes right by this beautifully preserved example of Roman culture (the villa is open March to October). The walk is mainly over flat farmland, going through the hamlets of West Burton, Bignor and Sutton; all have lovely old houses whilst at West Burton in particular you will pass by Cookes House. See it to believe it and it has as a companion a Lebanon cedar, a veritable giant.

Although the walk is flat, in the area of the mill ponds between Bignor and Sutton (see sketch map) during the winter you will need good footwear. It can be—for a short section here—very wet and muddy.

The parking area for this walk is in the old road layby on the A29, London to Bognor road, at the bottom of Bury Hill; the second turning on the left (coming from the south, first from the north) past the turnings to Bury and Bignor. There is unlimited parking. The walk starts at GR(197)000135.

Walk up to the blocked southern end of the layby at the nursery establishment of H. Bollam and Son, turning right into the farm track at the house. In a few yards, as the track bends right, walk straight ahead to go over a stile at a steel gate, going into a field (the footpath sign is on the other side of the A29 for this path!). Coming to another stile, the path continues between fences and a copse. In only a hundred yards or so down on your right in a little woodland glade, is a memorial stone to Fred Hughes and his wife Winifred, farmers in this district. You may want to go down and read the inscription on the stone; Fred chose this spot and in spring this glade is a delight, full of spring flowers.

The path continues and descends through a wood, coming to a stile—go over it and cross the few yards of the intervening field to the stile opposite. Cross over it at the footbridge and bear half right in an open pasture to a steel gate. Go over the stile here. There is also a two-way footpath sign at this location. Now, in this field with the tree hedge, fence and stream on your right—continue along the field headland and, reaching a two-way footpath sign go over the double stile into another field. With the fence, hedge and stream on your left follow this field headland to reach a timber power pole close by on your right. A two-way footpath sign at a steel gate is now ahead; go over the stile here into a broad enclosed track. With farm buildings and 'Martins Orchard' bungalow on the right, come out onto a lane and turn left. Pass on the left Cokes Cottage, and in a few yards beyond no doubt you will stand and admire the grandeur of Cookes House and its sentinel cedar. Coming to a lane junction, turn right into it, shortly to turn left at another junction, opposite Orchard End.

Continue down this lane to a third junction and turn right into the lane marked as a cul-de-sac, passing a house, Flints Orchard, on the right. Continuing along by its wall, come to a three-way footpath sign. With the old house of Fogdens on the left, walk ahead (with the stream on the left). Go over a footbridge—the stream will now be on the right, whilst the path continues through a copse area and the mill pond (dry). Coming to a clearing, bear to the left, with a hedge on your left. At a two-way footpath sign go over a stile into a cultivated field. Keeping the hedge and stream now on the right, walk along the field headland; West Burton and Bignor Hills are on the left. Coming to a two-way footpath sign, turn right. Going over a footbridge and stile into a large field (keeping a deep drainage ditch on your left), your course is directed into a wide track which runs the whole length of the field. With Jays Farm to the front and a cottage on the right, your way is out onto the lane, almost opposite the entrance to the Roman villa; turn left.

With the entrance to Jays Farm on the left and with Stane House on the right at a lane junction, continue ahead. Still in the lane, round a bend to pass by, on the left, the ford (bet you can't resist it) and a row of stone cottages. Going uphill with ·a red brick house on the left, turn left at a footpath sign (which is buried in the hedge). Go through a wicket gate—the house is now above you on the right. This path is now on a steep grassy bank with the mill stream below on the left. *Note* you are about to come to the area of The Four Mill Ponds which, in winter, is very wet. The path continues with an iron fence on the left and descends to a footbridge going through a copse, with a pond to your front. At a two-way footpath sign turn left. Go over another footbridge, coming then to a two-way footpath sign where you turn left to go over a footbridge and stile into an open field.

Walk up the rising ground to a line of trees and with a power line pole close by on the right, walk on to another stile into a cultivated field; once in it, turn right and immediately left. Still up the rising ground of this field, above which are the house roofs of Sutton, go over the stile on the other side of the field into an enclosed path which will come out onto a lane. Opposite is *The White Horse* pub.

With it behind you, walk into the lane to your front, signposted to Bignor and The Roman Villa. Continue on the lane passing Bignor mill and ponds on the right—there is a steep rise in the lane and you will then pass Bignor parish church. You will shortly reach the buildings of Manor Farm, also on the left. Coming then to a bend in the lane, walk straight ahead; a footpath sign will be on the right. Pass between some buildings of Manor Farm on a broad, muddy track. Directly to the front will be the thatched buildings housing the Roman villa. Keeping the houses and hedge to the right, turn left onto an enclosed track which will shortly meet with the Roman villa entranceway. Whatever your decision to call there or not, either continue straight on to Hadworth Farm on the signposted path or turn left onto it when leaving the villa.

On reaching Hadworth Farm, the footpath signs will direct you around the buildings and with them on your right turn left onto the farm track.

Continue along this track and where it bends to the right, at a two-way footpath sign, turn left into a grassy footpath. This will come to another two-way footpath sign—turn right into a woodland path which eventually will come out onto Bury Road (lane). Turn right and in a few yards, at a footpath sign, turn left. There is also a sign here—Kymber House and Cottage. Continue down this track to a three-way footpath sign and with Hale Hill Farm on the left, walk ahead. A succession of footpath signs will direct you through a wood and the short path will terminate at a stile with a footpath sign. Go over the stile and turn immediately right and the wood, of course, will be on your right. Walk the short distance to the fenced corner of this wood and turn right again. There are the remains of a stile here. Walk on with the wood still on your right, reaching a three-way footpath sign, and turn left to go over a stile. With a wire fence on your left, walking under power lines, you will see clearly a footpath sign on the other side of the field at a hedge. On reaching the sign, go down a bank, over a footbridge and stile into the next field. This leads to a collapsible (Sussex) gate. Go through it (please re-erect it behind you). The path will head towards two very large gateposts across the field and suspended between them is another Sussex gate. You will find, on going through into the next field, that the reason you could not see a footpath sign is that it is hidden by the bulk of the left hand gatepost—OK if you're walking the other way!

The buildings of South View Farm are now in front and you should aim to have all the buildings on your left including a big silage pit. Walk to a hedge beyond it where there is a two-way footpath sign at a footbridge and stile—go over them and turn left into a field. Now, with all the buildings of South View Farm on your left and a brick and white panelled house, Coachman Cottage, in a corner of the field to your right, walk towards it, and just beyond in the roadside hedge, is a steel gate. Go over the stile there and turn right into your parking layby.

THE MARDENS

WALK 14

★

9 miles (14.4 km)

Maps 1 : 50.000 scale 197. 1 : 25.000 scale SU 61/71 and SU 81/91

Another all day walk, which not only has superb countryside to commend it, but also passes by four old and historical churches, West Marden being the odd one without its own church—so allow yourself plenty of time. This is over lovely rolling downland with the route going through villages, farms and woodland. There are no steep hills. After lunch if you have to pause on the mile long lane climbing from West Marden to Locksash Farm, you will have good views. The paths and tracks are usually dry and firm.

There is plenty of parking space at the start of this walk on the very wide, long roadside verges at the junction of the North Marden road with the B2141 Chilgrove to South Harting road. This is about 5 miles north of Chichester and a similar distance from South Harting; the location of the parking and starting for this walk is GR(197)819162.

Assuming you have parked on the grass verge of the B2141 road as indicated by the sketch map, walk into the North Marden road and only a short way from the junction you will see the church and Meredon Farm. Almost immediately turn right into the farm and church entranceway. There is a footpath sign here. If it is your intention to call at the church, then as you approach the farmyard, walk into the fenced path leading to the church.

On leaving simply go out by the iron gate opposite the porch and into the farmyard. There is a two-way sign on the right, turn right and facing you will be a steel gate. Turn left through another gateway and walk down the descending headland of the field, with a fence, hedge and trees on the right. At the bottom of the field, go over a stile with a two-way sign on the left. Turn left into a narrow field—there will be trees and a fence on the left, with trees also on the other side of the field. Walk on for about 250 metres along the headland and turning right, walk to a gate in front of you on the other side of the field. Go over a stile and with a two-way sign here, bear right, then left to have a hedge on your left. Continue up the headland with trees in front and go by a ruined stile with a three-way sign on the left. Walk straight ahead—the trees and hedge will still be on the left. With trees again also in front, the path will go over a crossing track. The path will now go between trees.

At the end of this woodland path, go over a stile at a three-way sign into a large field and bear right to have the landmarks of Telegraph Hill and the reservoir on top of Appledown to right and left respectively. Once you have topped the rise in this field you will be approaching a fence; you will then see a stile and two-way sign. Go over the stile and with fence and hedge on the right, walk down the headland. On your left is Fernbeds Farm. At the

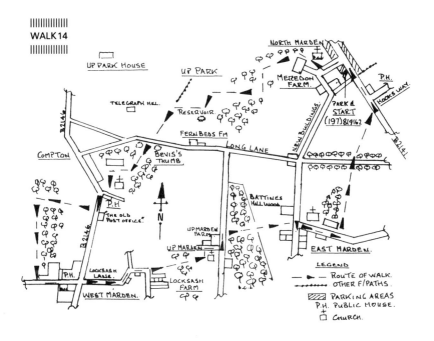

NOT TO SCALE.

bottom of the field go over a stile to your left and, going over a second stile in front of you, turn right. In a few paces left is now a fence and a wood on your right. Walk along the headland and go through a wide gap in a hedge, a three-way sign is on the right—turn left onto a wide farm track.

Continue on down the track, and coming to Long Lane, go across it. With a footpath sign on the left, there are two very wide distinct tracks here, take the right hand one. This is the area of Bevis's Thumb burial mounds. With woods on the right, the track will go through a gateway then continues through thick woodland. After some way it comes to a three-way sign on the right. Turn right and here go over a stile. The path goes across a field to a stile and footpath sign on the other side. Go over the stile into the stock yards of Compton Farm—the church and other buildings of Compton village are now in front of you. With two gates on the right, go over a stile at a gate to your front. Bearing left, go over the next stile at a gate, a three-way sign is on the left. Now on the farm track, continue the short way to the village street. The church is a short way to your left, a beautiful building to visit. To your right you will see Compton's pub.

With the pub on the left, turn left onto the B2146 road. Keeping to the left hand pavement walk on down the road and with The Old Post Office, a house, on the left, cross the road and go over a stile at a footpath sign and bear left. Walk across this field to the pine wood now in front of you, 'West Hanger'. Go over a stile and through the trees and, going over the next stile at a two-way sign, continue into the next field. The path bearing half right is heading towards a storm damaged wood. As you approach you will see a deer proof fence has been erected to protect the newly planted trees. Set into the fence, on both sides of this area, are large deer proof gates.

Using the first gate, walk across the area and go through the second gate. There is a footpath sign here. Walk into an open field—to your left is a grid power pylon with another further on to the front. The path continues over the field and then, with its corner in sight, there is a large iron tank on the left and four-way sign on the right. Go over a stile to bear left, then right onto a descending track to an iron gate. To the left of this, at the bottom, go over a stile at a three-way sign and turn left; the woods of Bottom Copse are on the left.

This headland will continue and, going over one stile and with trees also in front of you, you will come to another stile and two-way sign. Go over this and the path now goes through woods. Going over two more stiles, and with the buildings and farm of West Marden appearing through the trees on your left, the path will merge with the driveway of a house on your left. This will then come out onto the village road. Turn left onto it. The road continues through the village. The *Victoria* pub is on the left, and just beyond are the village crossroads.

Cross over the road and walk into Locksash Lane, signposted to Locksash. The metalled lane will climb and continue for about a mile. You will first pass, on the right, a large modern house, then Locksash Farm house also on the right. With farm buildings now in front of you, walk through double iron farm gates; there is a footpath sign here. Continue through the farmyards with the buildings on your right. Having passed the last one, the track now bears to the left and descends through woodland. Coming to a fork, take the left hand path; a two-way sign is on the left. This track will then come to a stile at a two-way sign—go over it and turn right. Soon you will come out into a field and with a wood opposite, walk across the field. Go over a stile, at a two-way sign. The path continues through Grevatts Copse and will shortly come to a crossing track. Turn left onto it. There is no sign here.

This track will then, in a few metres, go by a two-way sign on the left. Ignoring all other tracks going off to left and right, you will come to a three-way sign on the right. Walk straight on, still through woodland. Shortly beyond go over a stile and turn right at a two-way sign. In front of you now is Upmarden church—your next landmark. Fence and woods are on the right. This headland will continue and you will lose sight of the church. Simply walk on around the headland where, at one corner, on the right is a two-way sign. Continue to the next two-way sign and go over the stile in front of you. With trees and hedge now on the left, walk on to the next corner of the headland and turn left at the two-way sign here. Upmarden church is now across the field to your right. With a hedge on your left, walk down the headland. Then going over a stile at a three-way sign, turn right onto a wide farm track. Very shortly you will have the sign to St Michael's church, Upmarden on your right. It is literally only a few steps away and is such a lovely old building.

Your route will continue on past the buildings of Upmarden Farm—now private dwellings, of course. On reaching the road, turn left onto it. Just beyond the buildings, turn right off the road into a signposted path where shortly beyond and coming to a fork at a two-way sign, take the left hand path. With a hedge on the right, follow the headland down and with trees in front of you, go through a gap. This path, which descends very steeply down through Battines Hill Wood, will pass by a four-way sign on the right. On reaching the bottom, go over a stile into a field. With hedge and trees now on the right, walk up the headland. Coming to a stile at a two-way sign go over it. Turn right into a large field, there is a fence on the right.

This headland will continue on, still with the fence on your right. Passing a two-way sign and also going by power line poles you will reach a two-way sign, go over the stile and bearing half right walk across this field to its opposite corner. You will be heading for a white painted house which you will see through trees in front of you. At the footpath sign go over the stile and turn right into East Marden village street. The village well will be in front of you, on reaching it turn left. St Peter's church is now on your left—a grand place to have a quiet rest with the end of the walk not too far away.

Pass the church on your left and bear to the left, then with Willow Cottage and the post box also on the left continue on. With the village sign, East Marden, on your right, turn left just beyond it onto a concrete roadway. This leads into a large silage store area, there was no footpath sign at the road. Now turn left out of the silage area into a farm track. About 10 metres further on turn right through a ruined gateway into a field. Trees and hedge will be on your left—walk up this headland to where the trees and hedge end abruptly. Walk straight on across the field to a line of trees in front of you. You will see the stile there (this is Long Lane). Go over it and the one opposite, having passed by a two-way sign in the lane. Come out into a field, on the other side of which is another stile set in a line of trees. Go over this stile and through the trees and with a two-way sign on the right, walk across the field to a steel gate on the opposite side. Reaching this gate turn left onto the roadside verge of the B2141. Pass the junction on the right going down to the *Royal Oak* pub at Hooks Way. You will then soon reach your parked car at North Marden.

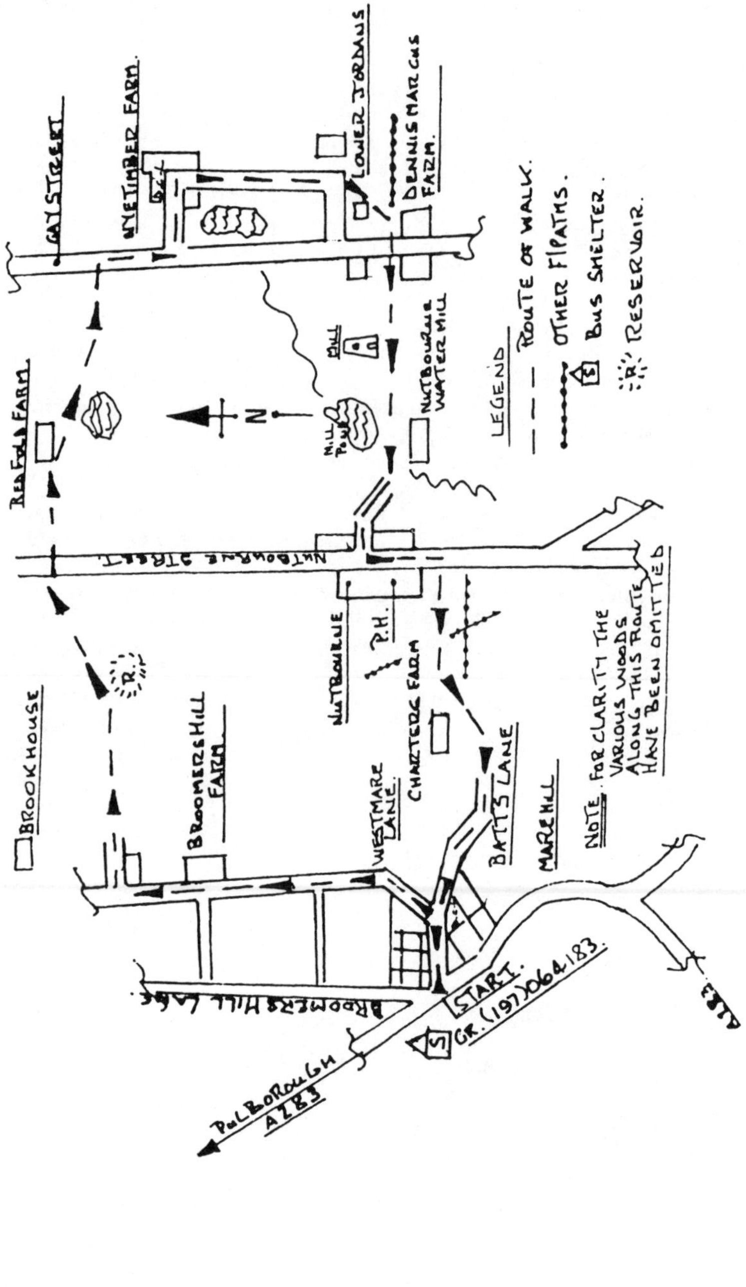

GAY STREET

NYETIMBER FARM.

LOWER JORDANS

DENNIS MARCUS FARM.

RAFELDS FARM

MILL

NUTBOURNE WATER MILL

N

MILL POND

LEGEND

— — — ROUTE OF WALK.
• • • • • OTHER FPATHS.
Ⓢ BUS SHELTER.
:R: RESERVOIR.

BROOK HOUSE

:R:

NUTBOURNE STREET

NUTBOURNE

P.H.

BROOMERS HILL FARM

CHANTERS FARM

WESTMARE LANE.

BATTS LANE

MARE HILL

NOTE: FOR CLARITY THE VARIOUS WOODS ALONG THIS ROUTE HAVE BEEN OMITTED.

BROOMERS HILL LANE

START.
GR.(197)064.183.
Ⓢ

PULBOROUGH
A283

A283

PULBOROUGH

WALK 15

★

4.6 miles (7.36 km)

Maps 1 : 50.000 scale 197. 1 : 25.000 scale TQ 01/11

The halfway point of this book with its last walk in West Sussex. You would be forgiven for imagining that, being so close to the Arun valley flatlands it could be uninteresting, but this is not so. At an elevation of only 290 ft (88 m) above the river flats, it is surrounded by the Downs to north and south, giving lovely views of both.

The terrain is all over farmland, across gently undulating open country-side that is well drained. Going through the lovely old farm of Nyetimber, a large area of its land now given over to vineyards, is together with Lower Jordans a little further on a delight at any time of year and especially so in springtime. There is the added interest of the route passing directly by the old watermill and remaining tower of the windmill at Nutbourne.

Pulborough has easy access from the west on the A29, or east from the A24 and both via the cross-country A283 road. The large roadside verge parking area, the start of this walk, is 1 mile east of Pulborough, on the A283 opposite the *White Horse* pub, with Mare Hill Antiques next door to it, on the north side of the carriageway. GR(197)064183.

With the *White Horse* pub and Mare Hill Galleries opposite to where you are parked, cross over the A283 road to bear right and walk into Batts Lane. Continue on until Batts Lane goes off to the right (this is the crossover point of your return journey). Here walk ahead into West Mare Lane; a four-way footpath sign is at this junction. Pass on by Kings Lane and Five Oaks and a two-way footpath sign on the right. Coming to the driveway of West Mare (it has twin concrete tracks) go down this driveway for about four metres and bear off to the right to go over a stile at a two-way footpath sign (*note* the short continuation of the driveway to a field gate is not a right of way). Walk to a two-way footpath sign ahead of you in this field and turn left at the sign.

The field path will continue, turning right at the next two-way footpath sign and, with a hedge and nurseries on the left, the path will lead up to a field gate with a stile and two-way footpath sign. Continue on the path beyond the gate, now in open fields but with a wire fence to the left. Go over a stile at a three-way footpath sign, and turn left on to a wide track. The buildings of Broomers Hill Farm are to your front. This path will continue up to the farm. At the crossing track and three-way footpath sign turn right to go by the farmhouse on the right. Just beyond turn left to continue still on the metalled farm track at a two-way footpath sign. At a bend in this track go through a field gate to your front, with a three-way footpath sign on your right. There will be a barn above you and on your right. Go through two sheep gates and turn right into a meadow. Now with a line of trees to the

63

right, walk along this field path and just before the end of this field turn right, going up steps set in the bank. Turn left over a stile at a two-way footpath sign.

Go over the stile at a field gate and two-way footpath sign now directly in front of you, into another field. A line of trees and a hedge will be on your left, at the end of which is a large pine tree (as you will see, the survivor of two). Turning left here at a two-way footpath sign, walk across this field keeping the reservoir mounds about 200 metres away to the right. On topping the rise in this field, you will see a solitary tree to your front with a footpath sign and stile beside it. Go over this stile and now bearing right across this field, you will soon have a field gate and footpath sign in sight in the opposite corner. Once through this gate, turn right onto the lane, turning left almost immediately into the track leading to Redfold Farm, which has a name board and footpath sign.

Walk along this track to come to a field gate and with Redfold Farm on the left at a three-way footpath sign go through this gate. Walking now down the descending field path and keeping a pond to the right, walk towards a four-way footpath sign set in a hedge. Go over a stream and stile into a field. Keeping a building ahead but to the right, walk towards it, then you will see a gap in the trees in front. Go through it and with a two-way footpath sign on the left, go over the stile at a two-way footpath sign to your front to turn left onto the lane.

Passing a pond on the left, turn right over a stile. A short way ahead at a footpath sign, and with farm buildings above you, go up this short field path and with another footpath sign at the top, turn right with the buildings on your left. Coming to a gate, go over the stile here onto a broad grassy track going through a large orchard and walk to a hut. On reaching it at a three-way footpath sign, turn left onto another grassy track. This will come to a two-way footpath sign. Go over the stile into a small field and with a building now on the left, walk on down the field, going through a gap in the trees. Go over the stile here and, going into this next field, make for the corner of it, keeping a field gate to your right. Go over a stile at a footpath sign to turn right onto Gay Street. The buildings of Crowell Farm are on the left.

Walk down the lane, passing on the left a bridleway sign at the entrance to Badgers Wood. Continue on the short distance to turn left into the entrance of Nyetimber Vineyard, as the notice here will tell you. Now on this wide, stony track and with the vineyards on either hand, continue on to the old farm (Nyetimber) buildings. As you will see this large farm was completely self-contained with all its own workshop facilities. With a modern building on your left, turn right on to the continuing farm track— perhaps you will see on your left a four-way footpath sign hiding behind a tree! With an old wall now on your right, beyond which is a large pond, and coming to a junction at a three-way footpath sign, continue straight ahead through a gateway. Pass on the right a modern house and just beyond at a junction, Lower Jordans, and with a two-way footpath sign in front, turn right onto a lane (Lower Jordans Lane). Just beyond and on the left is the farm track leading to a large barn. Turn left into the farm track and, walking between the barn on the right and another building now on the left, continue on beyond them into the field. In the opposite right hand corner you will see the buildings of Dennis Marcus Farm.

Walk down the field path. Just before reaching the farm buildings, in the hedge on the right, is a footpath sign. Go over a stile and down the stone steps set in this bank, and with a two-way footpath sign at the bottom, walk across Gay Street into the driveway directly opposite Stile Farm Cottage. At the end of the short driveway and garden go over a double stile at a two-way footpath sign, to go over another stile a little further on. This enclosed path with cut down poplars on the left and wire fence on the right will bring you to another stile. Going over it the right of way now turns left and right here, ie going into a field with the poplar trees on the right. Walk along this field (part of a market garden) with the remaining tower of the old windmill on the right, set in an orchard.

At the other end of this field at a two-way footpath sign go through a gateway to bear left onto a farm track. On your right will be the entrance to Nutbourne Manor vineyard. This track carries on and bearing right it will descend to the buildings of Nutbourne (water) Mill. With the mill pond in front, turn left and walk on by the mill buildings on your left. Coming then to a large thatched house on your right, continue on the lane and with a footpath sign to the front at a lane junction, turn left. On reaching the junction with Nutbourne Street and with Camber House opposite, turn left.

The *Rising Sun* pub is already in sight. The walk continues down The Street, passing on your right Mole End and The Drovers. At a public telephone kiosk and footpath sign turn right into Marsh Farm. Only a short way down its track and on the left set in a fence is a two-way footpath sign. Go over the stile into a large field. A short way ahead is a four-way footpath sign, go by it on your right and over an earth bridge across a ditch. With another three-way footpath sign well in sight to your right, close by a tree also in the same field, carry on up the field to a gate ahead which is clearly in sight. Go over the stile here at a two-way footpath sign and with a large shed on the left and a house on the right, walk between them. Coming to a gateway at a two-way footpath sign, walk now into Batts Lane, which will continue on with dwellings on either side. You will, of course, recognise its junction with West Mare Lane and turn left onto the continuation of Batts Lane. The short distance left will now take you back to your car on the A286 road verge.

||||||||||||||||
WALK 16
||||||||||||||||

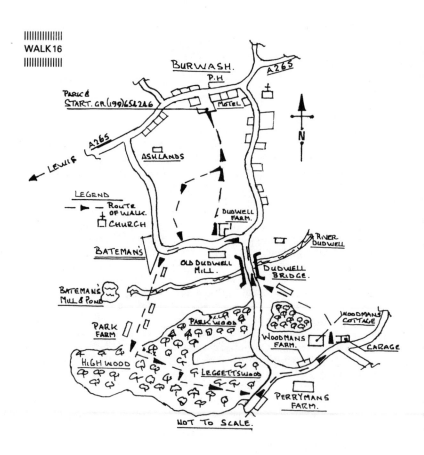

BURWASH.
P.H
A265
PARK &
START. GR (199)651246
MOTEL
A265
LEWIF
ASHLANDS
LEGEND
ROUTE
OF WALK.
CHURCH
DUDWELL
FARM.
RIVER
DUDWELL
BATEMANS
OLD DUDWELL
MILL.
DUDWELL
BRIDGE.
BATEMAN'S
MILL & POND
WOODMANS
COTTAGE
PARK WOOD
PARK
FARM
WOODMANS
FARM.
GARAGE
HIGHWOOD
LEGGETTSWOOD
PERRYMANS
FARM.
NOT TO SCALE.

BURWASH

★

4 miles (6.4 km)

Maps 1 : 50.000 scale 199. 1 : 25.000 scale TQ 62/72

This picturesque tree-lined village was described in *History of Sussex* 1870 as 'notorious for the lawlessness of the lower portion of its population, and scarcely safe for a wayfarer to pass after night fall'! As with several of these walks, this starts from the village car park, with field paths going to Bateman's, Rudyard Kipling's home. Now owned by the National Trust, the house and gardens are open to the public, 11.00 am to 5.30 pm five days a week (closed Thursdays and Fridays). We would quite understand if you were seduced from the walk by this beautiful place. The route of the walk across fields through farm and woodland is a delight, but you need good boots or shoes—there are three short sections of wet and muddy paths.

Burwash lies directly on the A265 road between Heathfield and Etchingham, south of Tunbridge Wells and north of Hurstmonceux and is, therefore, easy to reach. The large free car park is next door to the *Bear Hotel*. It is from here that the walk starts at GR(199)654246.

The waymarked path goes down between the toilet block of the car park and the *Bear Hotel*. Leaving the buildings, the descending path continues to a stile with a waymark. Go over the stile, the path still descending down a headland with trees on the right. With a footpath sign on the right, turn right going over a make-shift stream bridge, then go over a stile. Now bear right across a field. The path is heading to a large oak tree, and with a two-way footpath sign on the right, go over a stile. The path continues into a cultivated field. Walk on down the headland, with oak trees and a hedge on the right. Shortly beyond the last oak, turn right and go through a 'squeeze' gate (two curved oak posts; one has a waymarker).

The path continues across this meadow and, with trees close by on the right, walk on to a pond on the right and go through a gateway. Now with oak trees and a hedge on the left, walk down this headland to a gate. Go over the stile, very distinctive in that it also has a 'dog gate'. Turn right onto the lane leading to Bateman's, which is now in sight.

Coming to a junction and with Bateman's opposite, turn left into the track signposted to Park Farm. Passing by Bateman's Mill and pond on the right, ignoring a way sign also on the right, continue to Park Farm. Coming to the last of the buildings on the right, the right of way goes through a gate in front of you, but the way ahead remains blocked. However, the farmer is quite happy for you to turn left through another gate (on your left), then turn right in the field and continue up the headland by the fence on the right. You will then pass by an area containing scrap farm machinery. It is from this point on that the footpath/bridleway resumes its legal course.

With 'Highwood' now on the right, proceed on up the field and reaching the top you will be confronted by a fence and woods beyond. To your left, set in the fence, is a wicket gate; go through it. This is the first of the wet areas and churned up by horses—no problem at all if you have the proper footwear. This track flanked by woods will, in a short distance, come to a crossing track. Turn left on to it. At this crossways there is a woodland fence-making workshop.

With this stony track descending, you will come to a junction. Walk into the grassy path directly in front of you, going into conifer woods. In only a few metres this will descend to an unbridged stream. Then, climbing up the opposite bank, the forest track continues. Where it levels out and appears to continue ahead by a large pollarded beech tree, the right of way turns right. You, of course, continue on this track, which will then bend to the left, and continue still through the dense pine woods. Then the forest track will be in mixed woods, many of which are windfalls and across your path but there is no major obstruction. This track meanders on for some way and will come out onto a wide track, a clearing almost. Coming then to a junction, turn left onto the wide continuing forest track which very shortly will bring you to a gate, on the left of which is a notice 'Leggetts Wood'. Go through the gate. In front of you is a farm and stables, turn left onto the road. Coming shortly to a road junction, turn right into the road signposted to Etchingham.

This road continues, first passing Perrymans Farm on the right and further on Woodmans Farm on the left. This will bring you to your next landmark, a cottage called 'Woodmans' which is opposite a road junction to the right. It is at this cottage that you turn left off the road between the building and its garage, to go through the hedge down steps in the bank. With the cottage garden now on the left, go over a stile in the hedge in front of you. Now in a field, go through the gate in front of you. Woodmans Farm and tennis courts are to the left. There were waymarkers on the gatepost. Make your way to two isolated oak trees in the field to your left and go between them. There is the stump remains of a third tree here. Bearing to the left away from the two trees you will then have a fence-contained wood on your right. Walk down by the trees and coming to a stile, go over it. The path continues through a wood in which you will have to go over a narrow stream. The path, going up a bank, comes to a stile with waymarkers—go over it and turn half right.

You are now in a very long meadow. The path runs the whole length of it and you should aim to walk across it diagonally to the opposite corner. As you go across, Burwash and the church steeple will be to your left. Coming to the stile in the opposite corner, go over it. The path continues through a small wood and you will come to a wire fence. There should, of course, be a stile here—the landowner has made the concession of providing plastic tubs of concrete as stepping stones over the wire! Go over this make-shift stile and now in a field with hedge and fence to your right, walk up the headland, at the top of which go through a gateway. On your left is a thick hedge whilst to your right, a short distance across the meadow, is a thicket wood contained by a fence. Bear to the right and walk over to it. Now with the wood and fence close by on the right, walk on by it and in about 50 metres, you will need to be vigilant. You will come to a stile on the right, partly obscured by thorn bushes. Turn right over the stile, and the path now continues through the wood. Again you may encounter muddy conditions underfoot.

This path continues with tree-lined banks on either hand and with buildings on the right; the path will converge on to their entry way. Bear left onto it and walk down to the road. Turn right, shortly going across the bridge over the river Dudwell. Turn left into the single track lane on the other side. Dudwell Farm and Old Dudwell Mill are now in front to right and left respectively. Only a few metres beyond the last farm buildings on the right, turn right. Go through a staggered gateway set in the hedge. The farm buildings are again on your right. This short path will come to a stile. Go over it into a field. With the fence and hedge on the right, walk up the headland; the farm buildings also are still on the right. Immediately beyond turn right to go over a plank bridge and stile. Turn left and now with a hedge on the left, the path continues up this field headland. After some way and then with trees to your front, bear left and go over a stile with the path carrying on through woodland. Here once again you may encounter wet conditions underfoot.

Coming to the penultimate stile, turn left over it into a field. With a hedge on the left, continue up the headland. You will soon recognise where you are—go over the last stile and into the car park.

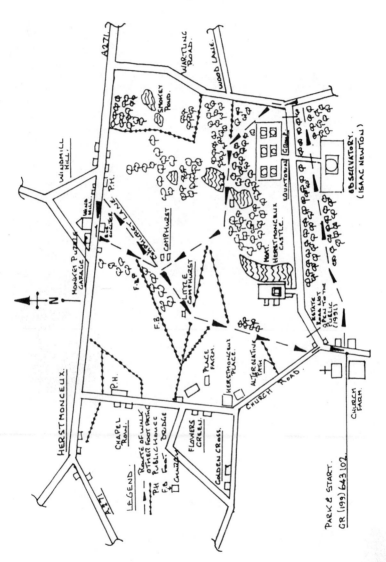

NOT TO SCALE.

PARK & START.
GR (199) 643102.

HERSTMONCEUX

WALK 17

★

4 miles (6.4 km)

Maps 1 : 50.000 scale 199. 1 : 25.000 scale TQ 61/71

Herstmonceux Castle, one of the first brick built structures in England, was built in 1440 at the then enormous cost of £3,800 by Sir Roger de Fynes (Fiennes), the direct ancestor of the present day Polar explorer, Sir Ranulph Fiennes. Both are the descendants of Count Eustache de Boulogne, the Norman who in 1066 despatched the wounded King Harold, for which act he was 'awarded' the Herstmonceux estate. At the present time, since the relocation of the Royal Observatory, there is no access to the castle, but on this walk you will get some good close up views of this wonderfully preserved building. An easy walk over undulating weald countryside, there are some very good views, and the going is on good firm paths. One bridleway can be very muddy but there is an alternative around this. You will find the beautiful old church of All Saints a delight and the canopied tomb of the Dacre (Fiennes) knights, a masterpiece.

There is no direct access from the south to Herstmonceux church from where this walk starts. To get to the location you must, from wherever you are travelling, get onto the A271 road between Hailsham and Ninfield and about ¼ mile east of Herstmonceux village turn south (right, if travelling from Herstmonceux) into the minor road signposted 'The Church and Flowers Green' (no mention of the castle or observatory). Continue on this road and the next signpost, on your right, will now direct you to 'Herstmonceux, Church and Castle, no through road'. You simply continue south and will then come to the large open area with the castle entrance on the left and church on the right, the distance from the main road being about 2 miles. Here you will find plenty of parking space, GR(199)643102.

From your car, walk south towards the entrance to Church Farm. On reaching it, a bridleway and footpath sign with two concrete waysigns will be on your right; turn left into the bridleway, with Church Farm House on the right. Bear left and go through a wicket gate marked 'Bridleway' beside a large iron gate. The main observatory (Isaac Newton) is in front of you. Coming then to the observatory service road junction, go through the timber gates in front of you marked 'Bridleway'. Now on a grassy track which will descend to a gate, go through it. Herstmonceux Castle will be in full view on your left. To continue, walk on to the four-way sign which you will already have seen as you came through the last gate and on reaching it continue straight ahead on the bridleway; the main observatory is still in front of you. Then going through a broken down gateway with a two-way sign on the left, the enclosed path ascends to a wicket gate.

71

Beyond the gate and now with a timber fence on the left and trees and bushes still on either hand, the six separate observatories known as the Equatorial Group, will start to appear on your left. (*Equatorial Group*, so called because the axis of the individual observatories were tilted to equal the axis of the earth for the observation of celestial equator heavenly bodies.)

Then coming to the junction of service roads for the installations, continue straight ahead still on the bridleway. Next to appear on your right is a large car park area. Coming to a wicket gate at a waysign, go through it and turn left onto Wartling Road. In only a few metres go by, on your left, the entranceway into Herstmonceux Castle Estates. A few paces beyond at a waysign, turn left over a stile. Also on the left is the curiosity of a stone marker 'Naval Ordnance Survey', one of two on this walk. Going at first through trees, the path will come out into a large field. On your left you will get a different view of the Equatorial Group. In front of you will be a line of trees in which you will see a very distinctive gap, walk towards it. On reaching it, the path continues into the wood and will shortly come to a waysigned stile—go over it and keep on the woodland path. Descending fairly steeply, the path goes over a plank bridge and bearing left beyond it come to a two-way sign on the right. Go through a pole gate here and turn left onto a wide bridleway; on your right is a large pond.

The wide bridleway, now climbing gently with hedges and trees on either hand, will come to a gate on the right. Go through the gate in front of you into cultivated fields. A well defined wide path goes through these fields and you will be heading towards buildings in front of you. Go through a gate and the field path continues. As you approach the buildings, these will be to left and right, respectively Little Comphurst and Comphurst. Could I suggest that you pause on this path to turn around to enjoy the Wealden views to the south with the single observatory structure still dominant, with a good view of Herstmonceux Place to the right. The field path will continue to a gateway. Go through it and turn right onto the metalled surface of Comphurst Lane. You will shortly pass by, on your left, a stile and gateway. You will come back over this on your return from Windmill Hill, whilst on your right you will go by an old brick building. The lane now continues to Windmill Hill, the buildings of which, including the body of the windmill, will soon be in sight.

Very soon the *Horseshoe Inn* will be on your right. The walk continues the few paces up to the A271 road. Turn left onto the south side pavement and you then have the sad sight of the derelict windmill standing in its original complex of restored and rebuilt buildings, now private dwellings. With a brick built bus shelter on your left, opposite is a filling station, Monkey Puzzle Garage, and Millers House in front. Turn left into an enclosed path—there is a concrete waymarker on the left here. Then coming quickly to a stile, turn right over it into a field. A fence and Allfree Wood will be on the right. Continue down this headland and go over the next stile. Now in a rough field, bear a quarter left, going over a railway sleeper bridge. Walk to a hedge in front of you in which you will see the next stile, which is a unique three step example; go over it. The next stile is obscured by rising ground. However the buildings of Comphurst and Little Comphurst are in view again and you should walk towards the building on your left and very soon a gate and stile will be in sight in a hedge. Go over the two step stile. Comphurst House is in front of you. Turn right onto Comphurst Lane. With Little Comphurst on your right and bearing left at the house, go over a stile at a gate. The route is now on a bridleway with hedges on either hand. Herstmonceux Place will soon come into view on the right and be with you for some way.

Now with open ground on the left and hedge on the right, come next to a gate. Go through it into a cultivated field. Continue along the headland, the remains of an old Victorian iron fence will also be on the right. Come to a series of gates, with a small group of trees on the left. Just beyond them one wide track bears to the right, the other turns left through a gate and over a field. In the introduction to this walk, I advised that if there had been prolonged rain, one section of bridleway could be very muddy and you might wish to avoid it; now you have come to the point where you can do so, by bearing right onto the wide farm track. Soon you will come to a gate, go through it and turn left onto Church Road. You will then, in about ½ mile be back at your car.

If you wish to continue on the bridleway, then turn left at the gate and walk up the rising ground of a field across which the track is quite clear, there are trees in front of you. Then coming to an iron wicket gate, the narrow path continues through bushes and trees to another wicket gate, beyond which you will come to a four-way sign on the right. Walk straight ahead, still on the bridleway. Then, coming to a third wicket gate at a waysign, go through it and down the short embankment and turn left onto Church Road. Here you will see the second Naval Ordnance Survey marker. From this point you will be able to see the castle lodge gates and the church and soon your car.

WALK 18

NOT TO SCALE.

LEWES

WALK 18

★

10.5 miles (16.8 km)

Maps 1 : 50.000 scale 198. 1 : 25.00 scale TQ 20/30, 21/31, 40/50 and TQ 41/51

Probably the most demanding walk in the series and for which you will need to be reasonably fit, together with keeping a weather eye on the forecast to pick a good day for this outing. There are long stretches of open Downland walking, magnificent on a good day, with unlimited views in every direction. The walk starts in a lane alongside Lewes jail, climbing up to the old race course and the battle ground site of Wednesday, May 14th 1264, when Simon de Montfort defeated Henry III and his son Edward. You will have no navigation problems on this walk, most of the way is marked with oak posts with carved out blue-painted direction arrows—a good system, no finger boards to go missing!

Access to Lewes is good from every direction and, assuming that you will be using the A27(T), turn into the A275 road off the roundabout west of Lewes town and soon Lewes Prison will be on your left. Coming to traffic lights, with Morris Road garage opposite, turn left, still the A275 road. Just beyond Spital Road on the right, turn left into a new road—The Gallops. Carry on a little way up this road and just before reaching the top and on your left you will see a large stables on the other side of the lane which runs parallel with this road. Park here, there is no problem in parking. To get onto the lane to start the walk, simply walk across the grass to join the lane at the stables. The location for parking and starting is GR(198)404102.

Just beyond the stables is a marker post—go through a gateway onto a chalk track, then coming to a two-way marker post, turn right. This narrow chalky path will continue on for some distance over the downside of Land Port Bottom; the area of the 1264 Battle of Lewes. You will pass by four marker posts along this path and the old race course buildings, now a training establishment, will come into view ahead of you. Coming then to a fifth marker post, bear left, then right, which will put you onto a broad, much used bridleway. The buildings are now straight ahead and you will then be walking between fences with all the buildings on the left.

With the last stables building on the left, and passing a marker post on the right, the broad bridle track continues to climb. The training gallops, the old race course, are on the left and contained still by its old concrete post fence. This will be replaced by bushes on either hand. On reaching a junction going off to the left, and passing (also on the left) another marker post, go through the gateway ahead. The broad stony track comes out onto open downland—there will be a fence on the left.

This track will then go by Mount Harry on the right and shortly beyond,

75

will come to a fork in the track. Here, with only minimal extra effort, could I suggest that you take the right hand branch to climb only a few hundred yards up to the trig point on Black Cap. At 678 ft elevation (206 m) this will give you the most magnificent all round views. Now coming off Black Cap, the obvious path will converge with the other one and ahead of you are stiles and gates. This is the junction with the South Downs Way. With a marker post now on the right indicating the South Downs Way ahead and to your left (ignore a wicket gate on the left), go through the gate in front of you and turn left onto the South Downs Way, which ultimately will lead you to the *Newmarket Inn*.

The descending path with fences on either hand and some bushes from time to time, will go through a gateway, having the acorn SDW symbol on it. This path will continue for some way, then coming to a four-way crossing track and marker post on the right, turn left to continue still on the SDW. With a fence on your left, passing a grid power pylon on the right, the Way (still descending) passes a gateway and marker post on the left. The track has become rough and stony and now beyond the fence on the left the track continues over Balmer Down and is completely open. Passing by a dew pond on the left, with the track now over grass, coming into sight and on your left is the next landmark, a large barn.

On coming to a stile and gateway continue beyond them and, with the path reverting to chalk, it is now approaching a gate leading to the barn. Turn right and go over the stile which has a SDW marker post. Walk up the downside to trees in front of you. Ashcombe Plantation is ahead and also a gate and stile. Continue beyond them into the woodland path. Now, with a flint wall on the left and going past a gate/stile and two-way sign, walk straight ahead on a grassy track between fences and shortly you will have the A27 below you. Then, with the *Newmarket Inn* and garage buildings in sight, on the other side of the road, and coming to a stile, go over it. Turn right and this will bring you onto the road verge of the A27 eastbound. I suggest that you walk the few yards to the SDW marker post, cross the road to the other marker post, turn right and carry on to the inn.

The South Downs Way continues on a concrete road between the inn on the left and garage on the right, also passing a Southern Water pumping station on the left. The roadway then goes under a railway arch. With marker posts on right and left, turn right. Once through the archway, the path now climbing and at first with buildings on either hand, will then go through a gate. With a hedge on the right, you will have the high ridge of the Downs above you and on your left, which you will soon be on. This path will continue to climb. Going through another gate, the hedge and fence on the right will give way to fence and the woods of Newmarket Plantation. However, the path will continue a little further down on the hillside and drawing away from the Plantation, will come to a field and wicket gate which will have been in sight for some time. There is a concrete SDW marker at this location.

Ignoring the gate on the right, go through the wicket gate and with a fence on the right, continue along the headland to a gate in front. With a marker post on the right, go through the gate and walk on to the next gateway—only a short way ahead. Go through it and there is also a stile and marker post here, still directing you on the SDW. There is also another post informing you that you are on Juggs Road, which comes up from Brighton to Lewes and was used by fisher folk in times past bringing fish to Lewes. As you continue along you will be able to see quite clearly almost the whole of your previous route, even from Lewes. There will be a fence on the right for most of the length of this path and eventually, coming to a gate, there will be a dew pond on the right. With marker posts directing the SDW to the right and Juggs Road straight ahead, go over the stile here, and continue on Juggs Road. The downland path now with a fence on the left, becomes a steeply descending stone and chalk track and some care is needed in negotiating it. At one point the Down on left and right is almost sheer and deeply terraced by rain. Kingston-near-Lewes is below you. Going through a gateway the chalk track will come to the metalled village lane and will make a junction with a road; Nan Kemps Corner is on the left. Nan Kemp was a witch, whose horrific reputation has long been used by parents to bring their children to order, 'behave or Nan Kemp will have you!'.

Cross over the road and continue into the opposite lane, signposted 'Juggs Road'. This will go by some houses on the right and then a stables and paddocks on the left. 'The Road', a chalk track, comes to a scrub wood and the track will go by this on the left, shanty stables are in this area. With Old Mill House on the right, turn left into the entranceway to the stables and just ahead at a gate and marker post, go through a wicket gate into a field. Bearing half left, walk down to go through a gate. Coming down this field you will, of course, have seen your next objective, the A27(T) road bridge. Once through the last gateway, walk across the bridge, going under a railway arch. Continue up this lane to come out onto the A275 road and with a two-way sign opposite continue into the lane signposted 'Houndean Farm'.

Go by Shepherd's Cottage on the right and coming to a fork in the lane, take the right hand branch. The other one goes to the farm. In only a few metres turn right (there is no sign here) into a clearly defined path which goes up the bank through bushes. It will very shortly make a junction with a crossing track. Turn right onto it and with the bushes becoming less dense, this track continues on. Houses will appear beyond the bushes on the right. Then the prison—and with a familiar marker post on the left, go through the gateway. The stables will now be on your right and from here you will have no difficulty in returning to your car parked in The Gallops.

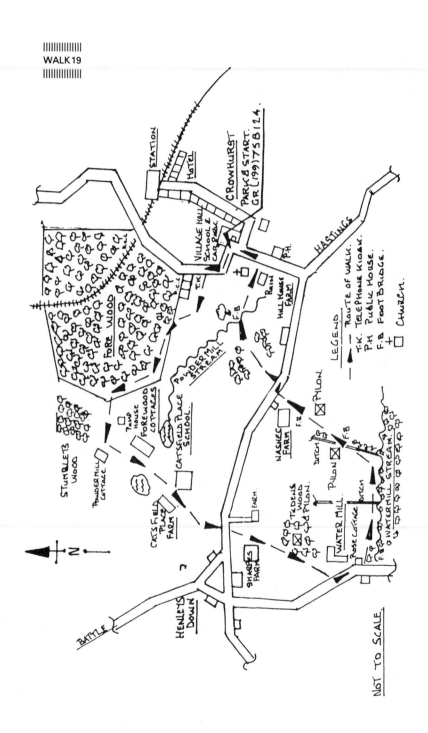

NOT TO SCALE.

LEGEND
— ROUTE OF WALK.
T.K. TELEPHONE KIOSK.
P.H. PUBLIC HOUSE.
F.B. FOOTBRIDGE.
☐ CHURCH.

CROWHURST

WALK 19

★

5.5 miles (8.8 km)

Maps 1 : 50.000 scale 199. 1 : 25.000 scale TQ 61/71

Only just to the south of the 1066 battleground Crowhurst village, farms and surrounding hamlets were totally devastated as a result of the battle but, of course, time has healed all those scars. On a more peaceful note, this walk has the distinction of going though the beautiful RSPB reserve in the large area of woodlands of Forewood. Here also the route is over delightful weald and farm country. The terrain is undulating and easy walking— during the growing season you may have to traverse two fields of standing crops but there are good land marks to direct you. A very interesting feature are the remains of the old manor house, a direct neighbour of the church; yet another interesting old building with the churchyard containing, on its south side, a 'remarkable old yew, 33 ft in circumference, and said to be 3,000 years old' (*History of Sussex*). Huge it is and, surrounded by its protective iron fence, old it certainly is; but whether 3,000 years old is doubtful.

Crowhurst is a fairly remote place to reach by road all of which are narrow country lanes and need to be negotiated with caution. Despite this the routes to the village are well signposted, from Ninfield, Battle and Hastings. The starting and parking location is at the village hall car park next door to the school and opposite the church. GR(199)758124.

From the village hall car park, go back to the road and turn right, passing St George's church on your left. You will reach, on the right, Court Lodge Cottages where, just beyond and standing on a green on the left hand side of the road, is a public telephone. Just before this, at a waysign, turn left and go through a gate into a large field. Trees with houses beyond will be on the right, and where both suddenly end at a waysign (also on the right), the path continues across open ground and you should bear left to the opposite corner of the field; coming to a gate in the field corner go over a stile. The path now continues through scrub woods and, coming to a gate, go through it into a large field. Making sure that you keep this gate directly behind you, walk across the field towards the trees, Forewood, now in front of you. Having reached the top of the rise in the field you will then see the gate and stile under the trees which you are making for.

Go over the stile, an RSPB notice is displayed here. Now on a wide woodland path you will shortly come to a pond where you turn left. Still on the wide woodland track which will follow the edge of the wood but is still among trees, the surface nature of the track is unmistakable so there is no chance that you might stray from it, and along its ¾ mile length it will undulate.

Suddenly, on the left, you will pass by another RSPB notice board. Then, going through a gateway and bridge over Powdermill stream and emerging from the woods, the path bears to the left and comes out into a field, to your left in a clump of trees you will see a brick pumping house. Walk across the field to trees on the other side and on reaching them you will go on to a metalled lane. Going to the left leads to the pump house, turn right onto the lane and you will immediately go through a gateway. Very soon at a lane junction and with Powdermill Cottage in front of you, turn left onto the other lane. In about a ¼ mile and then going through a gateway, Forewood Cottages will be on your left and just beyond their two garages the metalled lane will end. Walk on now into a wide grassy track going between trees. Go through a gateway into a field and with trees to the right, walk down the headland. On rising ground in front you will see the buildings of Catsfield Place School and farm. Do not walk the entire length of the field headland, you will quickly detect where you must bear to the right to get back onto the track which will continue between trees.

The track will come out into a small clearing and make a junction with a crossing track. Bear to the right and this will lead to Catsfield farmyard. You will continue away from the farm on a concrete paved track. Catsfield Place School is on your left. The farm track will make a junction with the loose stone driveway into the school. Bear right and follow the driveway down to the road. On reaching it, cross over the road. Without the luxury of a waysign to direct you, do not walk into the concrete driveway leading down to a large house but walk through a gateway to the right of it into a cultivated field. You must make sure now to walk to a line about 45° from where you are, making for the south west corner of the field. Depending on the time of year, you may have to walk through a standing crop. As you continue across the field trees to left and right will come closer and there, in the corner formed by the trees, you will find a dilapidated stile—go over it into a pasture. Now, on your left is a bank, fence and trees. Following this closely, walk on down the headland, then coming to an opposing hedge and fence, bear to the left and go over the waymarked stile into a field. In front of you now is a wood and a power pylon beyond. Aim to keep both to your left and then with Tildens Wood now close by on your left, you will come to a waymarked stile. You are now directly under the grid power lines.

Go over the stile and the path continues through Tildens Wood. Ramshackle out-buildings will appear on your right and then a house. Here you will be forced to turn right into the garden (the right of way) of the house and attached to a greenhouse is a yellow chevron way marker directing you left. Then going around a shed and coming to a stile, go over it and turn left onto a road. Walking towards houses in front of you, the site of the old watermill, continue on to have Rose Cottage on the left and here keep a sharp look out, there is no way sign here, and only just beyond the end of the cottage and set into its garden wall are some steps. Turn left here and go through a DIY gate and down steps on the other side. Now in a narrow fence-enclosed path, pass on the right a very attractive garden, and beyond go over a plank bridge across Watermill stream. With large cultivated fields to your front, bear right, and as soon as you can (with trees on your right) walk onto the bank path running above and parallel to the Watermill stream. You will need to watch your footing in places along this path; it's a long drop to the stream below! The fields are on the left.

This bank path will continue for about ½ mile and your way will be obstructed by a deep ditch which you will have to scramble across. Having done so, continue still along the bank path.

After a further ¼ mile beyond the last ditch you will be forced to turn left by trees and another ditch which will be facing you. Thus, having turned left, these will be on your right with the fields still on your left. Now walking up the headland you will be approaching a grid power pylon and lines. Just before reaching the pylon and lines you will see, down on your right and partially collapsed into the ditch, a railway sleeper footbridge. Turn right, go over this and the broken down stile in the hedge. You are now in a very large cultivated field and, depending upon the season, you may well have to 'first foot' through standing crops but again directly in front of you is another power pylon in the field and simply walk towards it. I suggest that you aim to pass it on your right and when you do you will then be approaching a hedge in front of you. On reaching it, turn left and with the hedge on your right, walk up the headland. At the top of this field and with another hedge in front of you turn right and go over a wired up gate and railway sleeper bridge. Now in another field and with a hedge and fence on the left, walk the short distance to a gate and turn left through it, onto a wide farm track, at the other end of which is Nashes Farm. On reaching the buildings, bear right, then left into the farmyard. Bearing right onto the paved farm track leading to the road, on the left at the corner will be Nashes Cottages and on the other side of the road is a waysign.

Turn right onto the road and cross over to the left and in only a few paces turn left into a track. Go through a gate into a field which is bordered by trees on either hand. Walk down the middle of this field but bringing the trees on the left closer to you and as you continue on the buildings and church of Crowhurst will come into view. About halfway down the field turn left to go through a gateway that has wire across it; the farmer being considerate enough to protect the wire with yellow plastic pipes, a good landmark. Here by the gate are two oak trees one with a twin trunk. Now in the other field and with the 'gate' directly behind you, walk on down the field. On reaching the rise in it you will see below you a gate in a hedge and just beyond another two gates with a footbridge between going over the Powdermill stream. Go through the three gates and beyond them is a large solitary oak tree, here bear right onto a wide grass track in this field. You will see the impression made by farm vehicles. Climbing very gently and reaching the top of the rise, the church and manor house at Crowhurst are in front of you.

Go through a gate and with the track bearing right, go through the last gate on this walk and you are now walking between the church, the manor house ruin and farm. On reaching the road, turn left. The school and village hall are then only a short step away on the right.

||||||||||||
WALK 20
||||||||||||

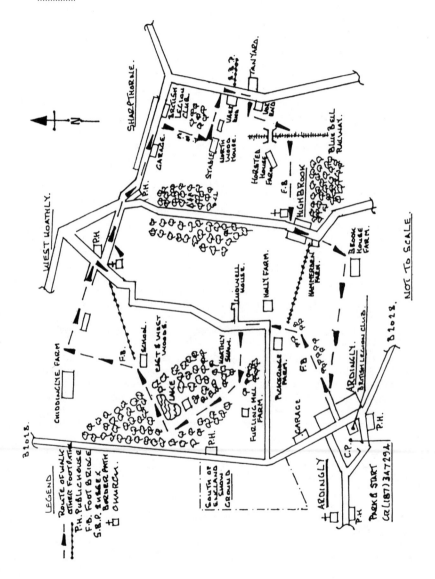

ARDINGLY

WALK 20

★

9 miles (14.4 km)

Maps 1 : 50.000 scale 187. 1 : 25.000 scale TQ 22/23 and TQ 23/33

Possibly the only walk in this series where I recommend a period in which not to undertake it. This, of course, is during the South of England Show at Ardingly—usually the weekend between the first and second weeks in June. But equally, I would recommend that you do the walk during the period of the last two weeks in May, in order to get the full beauty of the rhododendrons, wild azaleas and bluebells during that time. In the same area, West Wood, there is a large population of deer. This is not a strenuous walk but over lovely undulating countryside with some grand Wealden views, on good, mostly dry, firm paths. The route is directed around St Margaret's church at West Hoathly from where, surprisingly, on a good day it is possible to see the Channel through the Ouse Gap (the Cuckmere valley) in the Downs to the south.

Ardingly is easily accessible from the Crawley area to the north and equally so from the Sussex coast towns and via the cross country route of the A272. The walk starts from the free village car park at Ardingly, just off the B2028 road behind the British Legion hall and opposite the *Ardingly Inn*. You might find the car park crowded during the week but there is plenty of on-road parking between the *Ardingly Inn* and the *Royal Oak* pub in The Street. The park and start location is at GR(187)347294.

To start the walk, go back onto the B2028 road and face north, ie walk towards the village service station, with the British Legion hall on your left. Just before reaching the post office, turn right across the road into the lane alongside the village shop, signposted High Street, numbers 28–60. Walk the short distance to a gate and there go through an iron barrel gate into a meadow; industrial units are on the left. The clear path across the meadow heads towards a line of trees. There is a fence on your right.

Go over a stile. Now with a fence on the right the path goes down through trees, and going through an old iron gate it continues down still with the fence on the right, beyond which is a large house (a landmark on your return). Then going through another iron gate, the path comes out from the trees into a meadow; on the right is a three-way sign. Bearing half left across the meadow and with trees to the left and front, walk into a corner formed by the trees. Here, forming an archway, is a broken deformed tree, still very much alive. Once through this natural archway, the clearly defined path goes down through a wood. Then with a hedge on the left and going by a large oak tree, bear left and go over a footbridge. With a two-way sign on the right, go into a meadow. The path continues along the headland with hedge and trees on the right. Then with a two-way sign on the right, go through a gate into another meadow with the hedge still on your right. Go through a second gate by a pair of oak trees. Now with Pickeridge and Holly Farms in front, continue up by a fence on the left to the third gate at a two-way sign. Go over the stile here.

Continue onto the lane going through Pickeridge Farm. This pleasant tree lined track then comes to a three-way sign. Bear left to come to a road junction with the various farm signboards and footpath sign on the right. Turn right onto the road.

Walk on up the road passing the entrance to Ludwell House on the right. Then passing a gate on the left, continue the few metres to a second gate, also on the left. Turn left and go through it into a large field and with a hedge on the right, very soon you will see an object in the field to your left. Walk towards it and you will find that this is a large plastic fish pond utilised for animal drinking. There is a two-way sign here. Now directly in front of you is a promontory of a large wood, Hoathly Shaw.

Be careful to have this on your right. Now with these woods on the right, continue along the headland and, cunningly concealed from the last sign is another two-way sign, on the right of course. Shortly beyond this come to a gateway, turn right through it and now this narrow woodland path descends to a timber footbridge. Go over it and through the gate in front with a two-way sign on the right. The woodland path climbs gently to reach a timber paddock fence with this on the left and woods still on the right. The path will continue to a large clearing, walk into it and turn right; now on your right is a three-way sign. Walk into the broad track directly in front of you. This is the woodland way through East Wood which contains the rhododendrons, azaleas and bluebells which really give a lovely display in their season.

This long path is clearly identified along its length by old concrete fence posts and then coming to gates on either hand. Leading down from the right hand gate is a flight of concrete steps, walk on. The path then descending goes down to a crossing track, with a three-way sign in front—walk straight ahead. Before doing so, however, you will see on your right the large area of the Chiddingly Lakes.

The lakes will be in view on your right for some way. Then at another crossing track at a two-way sign, continue straight ahead. Here there are clear water springs. Now the track will continue uphill; on the left among the trees is a deep ravine with huge outcrops of stone. Suddenly there will be a building in front, part of Philpots School. Here also is a two-way sign. Turn left off the track into a very narrow woodland path, then going over a footbridge across the ravine with a two-way sign on the right the path climbs up to a footpath sign. Go over the stile here into a meadow with trees on your left. Walk up the headland and with a gate and two-way sign on the left, go over another stile and turn right. Still with trees on your left and coming to a gateway facing you at a two-way sign, turn left. Go over a stile and piank bridge, then cross over a railway sleeper bridge with the path going through a small wood. Go over another stile at a two-way sign and almost immediately go over yet another one. A gateway is on the left here. In this large meadow walk towards its single occupant—a Californian Redwood. Pass by it on your left then walk to the field gate in front of you. Go over the stile here.

Chiddingly Farm and house are now in sight across the field. Go through another gate and walk through the farm. Where the farm track makes a junction with a concrete roadway at a three-way sign on the left, turn right onto the road, which will continue by Chiddingly Hall and gardens on the right. Where the roadway bends to the left, walk straight ahead; there is a two-way sign here. Then going through a gateway into a large field, continue on the headland with a hedge on the left. Go over a stile at a gate and two-way sign. Still with trees and hedge on the left and coming to another gate, go over the stile there.

Now West Hoathly village and its church steeple will be in sight. The path will go by a two-way sign and through a fence where shortly beyond you will come out onto the West Hoathly road opposite *The Cat* pub. Turn right here and go through the church lychgate. The church is really worth a visit, but you are very close to one of the best views in Sussex . . . continue on round the church on the brick path, go down some stone steps and turn right then left. On your left is a seat with a tablet above, about the view to the river Ouse valley gap in the distant Downs.

Return to the second set of steps, at the top of which turn right and leave the churchyard through a wrought iron gate. Turn right onto the road. Continue on past the entrance to Glebe House and about 30 metres beyond turn left across the road to a safety railing and go up by the concrete steps in the bank. At the top at a two-way sign turn right onto a tarmac pathway. Continue on this path which will bring you to a car park and picnic area. Cross over the entranceway and shortly beyond go down a concrete stairway onto the road. On your right is the *Vinols Cross* pub, at a fork with the Turners Hill and Forest Row Road.

To continue the walk, cross over the road to the opposite pavement, now the pub frontage will be on your right. Walk on down the road and very soon you will be opposite the Sharp Thorne service station and the British Legion Club. Cross over the road and, although there is no indication that it does so, the right of way continues between the service station and the club building, which is on your left. Once into the club's rear car park area you will see, on your left, a footpath sign with the legend 'Sussex Border Path 1989'. This is the first of a series of such signs you will encounter which I will simply refer to as SBP. A narrow hedge-enclosed path leads away from the car park, and coming to a two-way SBP sign, go over the stile into a meadow. You will see Highbrook church steeple on the skyline to your right.

With a hedge on the left, walk down the headland and coming to another two-way SBP sign, go over the stile and the one opposite. Continue across this meadow to the stile in sight on the other side, also with a SBP sign. Go over this stile and turn right over another one. Now with woods on your right, you are again in a meadow. Drawing away from the woods on the right, walk up the meadow to go between a single tree on the right and two trees on the left. You are now heading towards trees in front and coming to a corner of the meadow, turn left over a stile at a SBP sign. Keeping a group of three oak trees to the left in this meadow, walk towards a stile and SBP sign. Go over the stile. The path continues into another meadow and buildings are to the right. Now heading between two brick buildings and with a gate on the right, go over two more stiles in front at a SBP sign.

The path continues into a field and, with trees on your right, walk on down the headland. Coming to a SBP sign, bear right. Go over a stile at a gate and with a SBP sign on the left, turn left onto a lane. On your right are the Gloverdale Stables. Walk on down the lane to the road junction and turn right, passing Tanyard on the left and the entranceway into 'Vaex End' on the right. Shortly beyond turn right into the entranceway into 'Vox End', a concrete waymarker is on the right. In a few metres, with a two-way sign on the right, turn left. With buildings on the left, go over a stile into a field. With a fence and hedge on the left, the headland goes between timber power line poles. Go over a pole gate and continue on the headland to go over a stile at a two-way sign. Now with trees and a deep ditch on the left, the field narrows and you come to a gate. Go over the stile onto a lane. Here on your right is a bridge over the Bluebell Railway Line where the lane continues to Horsted House Farm.

Cross over the lane and go over the stile now in front of you. With the Bluebell Railway track and a fence on your right, walk down this headland to the next stile in the fence on your right (please observe the warning notices). Go over this stile, cross over the rail track and go over the opposite stile. Now in a meadow, Horsted House Farm is to the right. Walk down the headland with a fence on the left and coming to a stile at a two-way sign, turn left over the stile. You will come shortly to a pole gate—go over it and descend steps let into the bank to a footbridge. The path comes away from the bridge and climbs up through woodland. Go through a gate at a two-way sign into a field. Walk along the headland with trees and hedge on the right. Then coming to a large oak tree and two-way sign, also on the right, go though the gateway in front of you.

A wide sand-based track leading beyond the last gate and still with a hedge on the right, it will continue on by High Brook church on the right. Then, with other buildings of the hamlet on the left, you will come to a metalled road. Turn left onto it. Hammerden Farm will be on the right and the Old School House on the left. Walk across the road to the village seat and sign. Go over the stile here at a gate and waysign. Continue down alongside a building on the right at the end of which, at a two-way sign, turn right over a stile. With a large house and garden on the right, walk on to the other end of this small meadow. At a two-way sign turn left and walk down the other headland. Go over a stile, Brook House Farm is now in front of you.

Continue down the headland of this field. There is a fence on the right. Turn right over a stile in the fence at a two-way sign. Just before the farm and in only a few paces, go over the opposite stile. Now on a wide farm track walk through a gateway in front of you. The track continues with fences on either hand, beyond which there will be an iron fence to your left. Coming to a three-way sign on the same side, bear half right across a meadow and, in the corner at a two-way sign, go through a gate. The path descends through woods and comes to a bridge—go through a steel kissing gate into a field. Now with a fence on the left, walk up this headland towards a large house. On reaching its fence on the left at a three-way sign, you will recognise where you are as being only a very short way from the village car park at Ardingly.

ALFRISTON

WALK 21

★

5 miles (8 km)

Maps 1 : 50.000 scale 199. 1 : 25.000 scale TQ 40/50

Alfriston, yet another 'deceased' port of Sussex which, in company with Arundel, is a honeypot for tourists. Please do not let this deter you for within a few moments of leaving your car, you will be in the midst of some of the most delightful and rural countryside in East Sussex. Although on almost flat ground, you will be surrounded with magnificent views. The walk is over good, dry, firm tracks and paths. You will be further delighted by the hamlet of Berwick, where the walk is directed through the churchyard and on to Alciston coming out opposite its lovely old pub, with the added attraction here of that ancient collection of buildings, comprising church, dovecot and tithe barn. I should not, however, forget to recommend that you should also visit Alfriston's church, 'The Cathedral of the Downs' (hopefully where you will park) and its neighbour The Clergy House, the oldest building owned by the National Trust.

Alfriston is easily accessible from all the major roads, the A27, A259, A22 and A267 etc. The walk is intended to start from the church green at Alfriston, but to secure a parking space there (free), you should arrive early. There are two alternative town car parks, both of which are well signposted. The one in West Street, which you will walk by on the route, is free, whilst the one opposite, on the east side of the road coming from the north into Alfriston, is a 'pay and display'. But wherever your parking venue, I shall ask you to start the walk from the church green at location GR(199)521020.

Leave the church green, taking the brick and cobblestone path alongside the United Reformed church and reaching the village street, turn right and walk up to the village cross. Here cross over to the opposite pavement and with the cross on your right and the *Smugglers Inn* on your left, walk directly into West Street, the lane directly in front of you, which in the next few metres will take you by the entry into the West Street free car park. It contains the restored flint one man 'lock-up', used to house unruly drunks for the night in times past. Go by West Close on the left and, the lane now ascending, passes by Sloe Cottage, then a crucifix shrine, part of the Sanctuary, all of which are on the left. Shortly beyond and coming to the junction with Winton Street, walk straight ahead into an unsignposted grassy path.

Your next objectives, Berwick church and hamlet, are straight in front of you across the fields. First passing by a ruined stile on the right, the headland path goes across three fields and continues with hedge/fence on the right. You will go over two double waymarked stiles, then another single waymarked stile and plank bridge. Beyond this the path comes to a wide

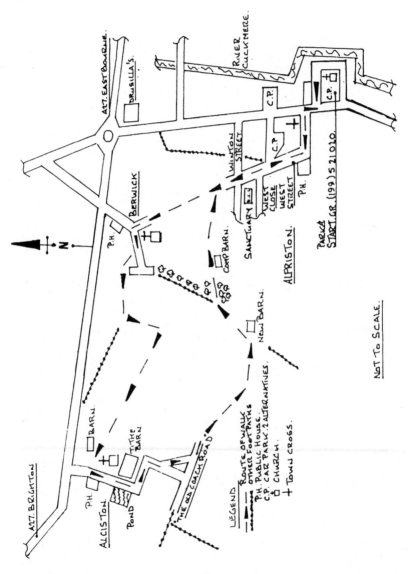

crossing track with Berwick church just beyond the trees in front. Turn right onto the track then, with a marker post on the right, turn left through a gap in the hedge and go through a wicket gate leading into Berwick churchyard—St Michael's and All Angels. The walk continues past the front porch of the church, down a flight of concrete steps onto a gravel path. Turn right, this will lead to the car park area for the church from which there is only one way out, onto a concrete lane. Turn right and this will lead to a road junction in the hamlet. The direction to the right will take you to the pub *The Cricketers Arms.*

The walk continues by turning left at the road junction (straight on of course if walking back from the pub). Now with Church Farm on the right, and coming to a crossways with an oak marker post on the left, walk into the concrete farm track—estate houses will be on the right and farm buildings on the left. With the concrete track bearing off left into the farm and with a marker post on the right, turn right into a cultivated field.

You will now see the buildings of Alciston in front of you, shrouded by trees. With hedge/fence on the left, the headland will bring you to a waymarked stile on the left. Go over the stile in front of you into another field and continue on its headland, still with hedge on the left. Go over two stiles with a plank bridge between, into a third field then, coming to a gate set in a hedge, go over it (literally) into a meadow and with a fence on your left, continue along this headland. Go through a gate and with a pond on the left walk up to a flint barn/stockyard on your right where, just beyond, is a waymarked stile at a gate. Go over the stile and directly in front of you is Alciston's pub *The Rose Cottage Inn.* If you visit this delightful place during the nesting season watch out for swallows zooming in and out of the porch as you go into the pub!

With the pub on your right, the walk continues on up the lane coming shortly to the three ancient buildings which are the highlight of this walk: the church, dovecot and the tithe barn. The church, regrettably, is the only building you may visit, a lovely dignified old place. However, you will be close enough to the other buildings to appreciate how important this totally self-contained establishment must have been in the Middle Ages, run then by a monastic order.

From the church, go back out to the lane and turn left. The lane continues around the farm and tithe barn on your left, and duck pond on the right. With the lane bearing to the left and going by a stockyard on the right, pass on the left a pair of old cottages numbers 48 and 49. The metalled lane will give way to a brick and rubble track, which, after climbing for a short way, will come to a fork. Turn left onto another wide track—The Old Coach Road. This mile long 'road' passing first on the right, New Barn, and with Berwick church on the left, will come to trees to your front. Where the track bears left to Berwick, The Coach Road goes straight ahead between trees into a narrow path. Coming into the open the path broadens once again to a wide track and passing by Comp Barn on the right, will then come to the crossway with Winton Street at the head of West Street, which of course, continues back down to Alfriston.

NORTHIAM

WALK 22

★

3.5 miles (5.6 km)

Maps 1 : 50.000 scale 199. 1 : 25.000 scale TQ 82/92

This old village, which bears the burden of the busy A28 road but from which you can quickly get away into its beautiful surrounding countryside is, as you would expect, greatly influenced by neighbouring Kent, with many lovely old buildings and oast houses. The most famous of these houses is, of course, 'Great Dixter', set in its lovely gardens which, no doubt, you will take the opportunity to visit. The house and gardens are open to the public daily—May to October (Monday and Bank Holiday Mondays excepted) 2 pm to 5 pm. Additionally, almost at the start of the walk you will go through Wildings Farm, the house of which has been completely restored. The terrain is almost totally flat through open pasture and farmland with a liberal sprinkling of native trees. As the walk starts so near to the church, I would suggest that you visit this interesting old building also.

Access to Northiam from north and south is via the A28 or A229 with the inter-connecting B2165 from the west. From the east the approach is on the A268 and then using the B2165. Similar to Burwash (Walk 16), there is a large free car park in the village situated just south of the pub and adjacent to the church, directly off the A28 road. It is from the car park you will start your walk at GR(199)829245.

Leave the car park by its only entry/exit point and turn right into the lane leading up to the church. On your left in the hedge is a stile; St Mary's church is only a few metres beyond this point. Turn left over the stile at a footpath sign and with a hedge on the right, continue down the headland to a stile. Go over it into a large cultivated field with a cleared footpath through the crop. Wildings Farm is in front of you. The footpath continues through paddock fences on either hand and will lead directly into the farmyard. With the restored farmhouse on your left, continue beyond it and, going over a stile, the path now has paddock fences again on either hand. Passing a pond and seat on the right, and going over another stile the path descends down into a small wood. An interesting point to note is that you will then go past, on the right, a 'Bodgers' Woodland Workshop—a fence and rustic furniture maker.

The path continues through the wood and you will have to cross over a narrow unbridged stream beyond which the path, now climbing, will come to some buildings. Here you will shortly join a metalled lane; on your right is a white waysign: 'public footpath to Northiam church'. The lane bends left then right, a green is on your left and houses to the right. You will then come out on to the A28 road—turn left and keep on this pavement.

NOT TO SCALE.

Continue on down the road, with a general store and off licence on the left. Pass this shop to Pear Tree Cottage, a Sussex timber clad house on your left. On the other side of the road are a pair of new red brick and timber clad houses. Cross over the road to them where, by the side of the second house, turn right over the stile set in the hedge. The path goes between the houses and hedges and comes to another stile—go over it. With trees and buildings on the left, continue on this headland to another stile in a hedge. Go over it and with a house to your front, Chapel Field Cottage, turn right onto Dixter Lane; a concrete waysign is on the road verge.

Continue up the lane to a junction and with a sign to Great Dixter on the right, bear left into High Park (Lane). Directly in front is the noticeboard for the house and gardens. If it is your intention to visit the house, then simply go through the gates and use the driveway, which you may do during the 'open' season anyway. If you do this walk out of season, then you are obliged to use the footpath to the right of the gates and signboards, signposted to Ewhurst. Using the path, it will come to a toilet block on the right. You are then obliged to join the driveway of the house and walk ahead to a gateway where there is a green waymarker 'To Ewhurst'.

Go over a cattle grid and, keeping the boundary hedge of the house and gardens close by on the left, Little Dixter is across the field to your right. The path direction is indicated by a wide swathe cut across the meadow. With a pond to the right and coming to a field gate with a marker post, go

91

over the stile here. With wood and hedge still on your left, continue down the headland of this meadow, coming to a field gate at the bottom on the left. Turn left through this gate. Now on your right is a stream and line of trees. In only a matter of a few metres from the gate, turn right and go over a bridge across the stream. Then only just beyond the bridge, turn left to go through a gap in the hedge by an old blackthorn tree.

You are now in a meadow with the stream and line of trees close by on the left. Carry on along this headland; it will continue for some way. You will need to be vigilant not to miss the substantial footbridge which will be on your left—turn left across it. Continue along the headland. Bushes and trees will still be on your left, whilst to the right in this field are timber power support poles. Coming to a gateway turn left through it and just beyond the gate, turn right. Now in a long, narrow meadow with the trees and stream on the right, continue down the headland. You will pass on the right, a ruined brick building from where you should be able to see the gates at the other end of the meadow. Walk towards them and go over the stile. A footpath sign is on the right, cross over the road here.

Now in front of you are the entranceways to Strawberry Hole Cottage and Strawberry Hole; a concrete waymarker is down on the left. Ignoring the driveways to the houses, turn left through an old ruined gateway and you will be on a narrow path flanked by trees; Strawberry Hole Cottage will be on your right. Then, coming to a stile with a field gate to the right, go over the stile. The path then goes across the meadow with trees to the left and power lines to the right, in only a short distance coming to a deep depression filled with trees on the left. In a hedge facing you, go over a stile at a three-way sign. You will see Northiam church steeple across the fields. The path continues on a broad track through a cultivated field. It is worth pausing and looking back at the picture postcard setting of Strawberry Hole with its oast houses.

The field path will come to the entranceway into Northiam's large sports field. Walk to the opposite end and go through the gateway at the A28 road. To your left is *The Crown and Thistle* pub, to the right is the car park only a short distance away.

BRIGHTLING AND 'MAD JACK' FULLER'S FOLLIES

WALK 23

★

3.9 miles (6.2 km)

Maps 1 : 50.000 scale 199. 1 : 25.000 TQ 61/71 and TQ 62/72

Brightling, a small hamlet south of Burwash, is dominated today as it was during his lifetime by John (Mad Jack) Fuller MP, 1757–1834, the son of a prosperous Sussex iron master. As far as it is known John Fuller did not pursue his father's commercial interests, much more likely he increased the family fortune with dealings in the City, but in any event he put his considerable fortune to very good use in providing gainful employment for the local population in the construction of his many building projects.

The 'follies' which surround Brightling include The Pyramid, The Tower, The Rotunda Temple, The Sugar Loaf, The Observatory (this is not truly a folly, but built by Fuller to satisfy his interest in astronomy), and last but certainly not least, The Brightling Needle. Of these extraordinary buildings and John Fuller himself, Geoffrey Hutchinson has produced an excellent, very readable booklet entitled: *Fuller, The Life and Times of John Fuller of Brightling 1757–1834* which is obtainable from the church of St Margaret and St Giles. The church is the site of The Pyramid—Fuller's tomb.

The route is circular, over easy undulating countryside. The going can be muddy after continuous rain, but do not be deterred. The Follies notwithstanding, the Wealden views are spectacular.

Brightling is situated approximately 5 miles north-east from Battle and 3 miles south-east from Burwash. There is adequate parking in a layby only a few yards into the Robertsbridge Road, just down from the church at GR(199)685209.

On leaving the church turn right to walk down to the road junction, crossing over it to walk through a wicket gate alongside an iron field gate. There is a low level concrete footpath marker here. Continue across this field to an opposing hedge, the views to the left are splendid. Go through a kissing gate set into the hedge. There is also a footpath sign here. The path leads on now with a hedge on the left, and across the open field on the right is a full view of The Tower set in its ring of sad storm battered trees. Come now to an opposing hedge, to go through it and then a kissing gate and immediately beyond turn right into an unmarked path which shortly reaches The Tower. Access is gained through a heavy iron gate. The inside of The Tower has been modified to give access to a viewing platform, above which is a steel ladder giving access to another viewing location from which to enjoy the splendid views.

Leaving The Tower, walk through the trees across an open field, through

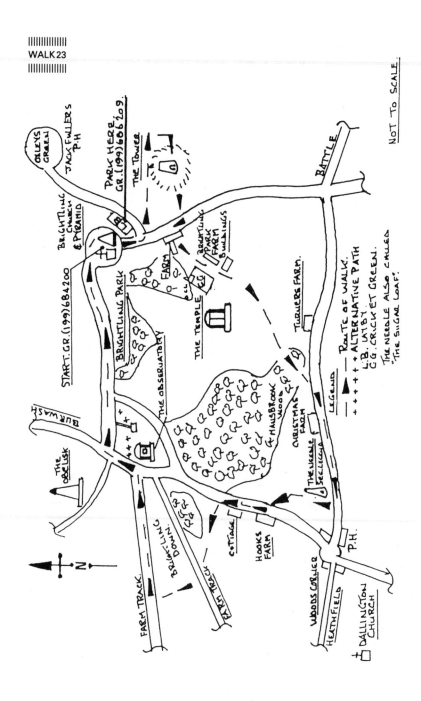

94

a gap in the roadside hedge and turn right onto the road. In coming down this field both The Rotunda Temple and The Sugar Loaf will be in view. In about 100 yards, turn left off the road and go through the stone pillared gateway into Brightling Park Farm and continue on the rough farm track to reach a field gate on the right; the track bears left to go through a gateway and on the right is a large pond. Next to appear on the right is Brightling's cricket pitch, completely enclosed by a wire fence. Beyond and to the left are farm stockyards and a stone building. Continue to the end of the fence and turn right and in a few yards the farm buildings will be on the left, with the stone buildings immediately on the left. The grassy track continues and goes through another gateway.

In only a short distance beyond the last gate and now in full view to the right, is The Rotunda Temple. This imposing building set on its vantage point of beautiful parkland, at 484 ft elevation (147 m), is not accessible by public right of way.

The wide track now enters a small wood and emerges onto open ground through a ruined gateway. Continue on the field path. Do not be deceived by a track which bears away to the right, but walk ahead on the descending path into Mansbrook Wood, crossing a brook with a ruined stone wall on the right. This path will shortly emerge onto a wide crossing track, turn left onto it. In about 50 metres, turn right into a dense, very dark and eerie conifer plantation. This woodland track will ascend and meet another crossing track. Turn left onto it where, in a very short distance, it will come to a pole gate. Climb over this and now come out into a field. Go left and then right to follow the field headland up to the road, which is reached through an iron gate with a footpath sign on the left. Turn right onto the road.

Now you will pass on your left, Hollihocks and Pelham Buckle cottages. The next buildings on the right are Bethlehem Cottage, Christmas Farm and Little Bryers restaurant and motel. The Sugar Loaf will now be in clear view—continue towards it and turn right onto the footpath to reach it. This folly built by Mad Jack to win a wager, represents the top 30 ft or so of nearby (but out of sight) Dallington church, and was at one time used as a residence.

The path continues north out of the enclosure. Go over the fence into a pasture field and walk towards the clearly visible pole hunting gate in the opposite hedge. Go over the poles into an enclosed footpath. At the bottom, on the right, is a gate and a two-way sign, turn left and in only a few yards, turn right onto a road. Opposite will be Hooks Farm house. Continue to walk north up this road to pass by a pair of traditional Sussex shiplap cottages where, shortly beyond and also on the left, turn left into a signposted footpath. Go across a large cultivated field. In case this path has not been reinstated after sowing (as was the case with the author), take care to bear to the left across the field to walk towards the extremity of a wood on the right, easily identifiable by an animal watering trough at the tip of the wood.

Bear right around the tip of the wood and the watering trough into another field, on the opposite side of which is a large solitary oak tree. Walk by the tree and across the next narrow field to go over a double stile with a plank bridge into another narrow field where, slightly to the left, go over another stile at which there is a four-way sign. On the other side of the intervening track, go over another stile and now walk up an area of open downland (Brightling Down); going under power lines make for a line of trees directly ahead—and there, set in trees, is a pole hunt gate (to the left is a large house). Go over the gate, on the other side of which is a clearly identifiable, wide rutted track leading through a devastated area of woodland (Upper Plantation). The tip of The Observatory will reveal itself on the right. The present track will then make a junction at a rough stone one. Turn right onto it.

Pause here for a moment and turn around and you will see The Sugar Loaf and Dallington church on the same ridgeway of hills—the significance of this will become apparent when you read Geoffrey Hutchinson's booklet *Fuller*.

Continue up the stone track and The Obelisk, known as the Brightling Needle, will soon come into view on the left. This also is not accessible by public right of way. Shortly beyond, the track emerges onto a road almost directly opposite The Observatory, now a private residence. Turn left onto the road and just beyond the building on the right is a field wicket gate. At this point you may take the short distance of a field path to the road junction leading back to Brightling or continue on the road to turn right at the next road junction, then to bear left into the signposted lane—to 'Brightling 1 mile'. The field path would have come out just above this point. This is not a very busy lane and continues (as do the views to the left) downhill back to the village. You pass Avenue Lodge on the right, the entrance to Mad Jack's home, Brightling House—sadly not open to the public.

I am indebted to Edward Shoosmith who wrote of John Fuller (*Sussex County Magazine* July 1933), 'May his soul rest in peace or travel happily over Elysian fields, for in Sussex he was a good man'.

SLAUGHAM

6.5 miles (10.4 km)

Maps 1 : 50.000 scale 198 or 187. 1 : 25.000 scale TQ 22/32

Though Slaugham (pronounced 'Slaffham') is very close to both Gatwick airport and the A23(T) London to Brighton road, this walk is set in beautiful wooded Wealden countryside over which, in the main, the paths and tracks are good and dry. The area abounds with ponds, lakes and streams, most of which were harnessed for their power by the old Wealden ironmasters. What a delight the two villages of Slaugham and Warninglid are—the former a favourite with Admiral Nelson, whose sister and her husband had a large farm here, but sadly the whole estate has been broken up. Nelson's sister and relatives on both sides are buried at Slaugham church (at the eastern end) in a large tomb and the old headstones with their picturesque language makes historical reading.

Slaugham has good access from every direction via the A24, A272, A23(T), A279, B2114 and B2115 roads. Doing this walk on a Sunday and intending to park in the large car park at the church, we found this already quite full at 10.30 am but there was no problem in parking on any of the adjacent roadside verges. Please do not park in the *Chequers* car park. The church car park location to start the walk is at GR(198 or 187)257281.

With Slaugham church at your back, walk across the road into the lane opposite, a cul-de-sac, and with *The Chequers Inn* on your left, continue up the lane to a gate. Just beyond it at a waysign on the left, turn left over a stile at a gate. The footpath is on a broad grass track going between a fence and hedge which, in a short way, goes into a wood. Here at a two-way sign and turning left, the path goes across a stream bridge and climbs up a short distance to a gateway. Do not be confused with other paths which have been created here. Go over the stile at the gate and the narrow path continues on for some way. Then, coming to the garden fence on the right of Poyning-shurst House, the path will come out onto Coos Lane (yes, that's its name!). Turn left. This quiet lane will continue on for about ¼ mile passing by large houses, notably Lower Ashfold, on the right. Then you will get a clear view of a large lake, Furnace Pond, on the right. At the crossroads, turn right, signposted to Horsham and Lower Beeding—Furnace Pond is still on the right.

Continue on the road and in about ½ mile, turn left into a lane marked as a bridleway. Going over a bridge, buildings will appear in front of you. Pass by on the left a half-timbered house then, coming to a fork with a two-way sign, take the left hand fork. You will see on your right, across the field, Bells Farm house. You will then pass by on the left Denmans Farm, where just beyond the metalled lane will end and a narrow path will be going between

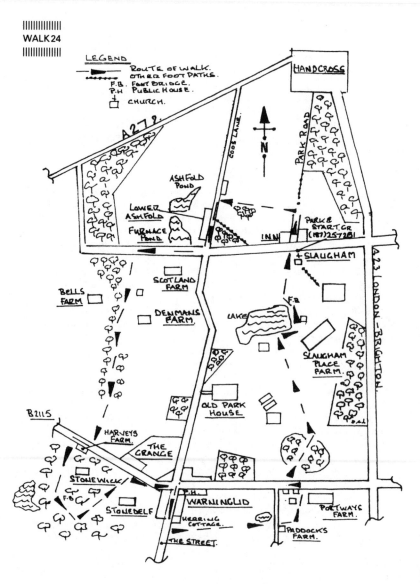

WALK 24

LEGEND

▶▶▶ ROUTE OF WALK.
•••••• OTHER FOOT PATHS.
F.B. FOOT BRIDGE.
P.H PUBLIC HOUSE.
⌂ CHURCH.

A279
HANDCROSS
PARK ROAD
COOS LANE
N
ASHFOLD POND
LOWER ASHFOLD
FURNACE POND
INN
PARK & START. CR.
(0187)25728
✝ SLAUGHAM
A23 LONDON - BRIGHTON
BELLS FARM
SCOTLAND FARM
DENMANS FARM.
LAKE
F.B
SLAUGHAM PLACE FARM.
OLD PARK HOUSE
B2115
HARVEYS FARM.
THE GRANGE
STONEWICK
F.B
STONEDELF
P.H.
WARNINGLID
HERRING COTTAGE.
PORTWAYS FARM.
PADDOCKS FARM.
THE STREET.

NOT TO SCALE.

98

a fence on the left and trees on the right. Climbing gently the path goes through a gateway where just beyond go through a gate into fields. Ignoring the wicket gate on your left, walk into the field in front of you. A hedge will be on your left, walk down the headland to go through a gate at the bottom of the field and with a waysign here, go out onto the road and turn right. Very soon Harveys Farm will be on your left. Turn left into the lane signposted to Stonewick. Then, with a two-way sign on the right and a gate in front of you, go over the stile. The lane of course, now on your left, continues to Stonewick.

The path will come out into an area which has been cleared and contains a stand of mature oak trees. To your left will be a building. The wide track continues to a two-way sign in front of you and with it on your left the track now goes into a wood. It will descend to a three-way sign, when a large lake is on the right. Turn left. Still on the woodland path and still descending, go over a rustic footbridge. Now with a two-way sign on the left the path will climb to a staggered gateway in a fence at a waysign. Turn right onto a wide track and almost immediately turn left at a three-way sign. Go through a wicket gate with a notice 'Public Footpath', which will continue into woodland. With an iron gate in front of you and a three-way sign on the right, turn left onto a climbing woodland path. With pines on the left and pollarded beeches on the right, the path climbs steadily uphill. Now with a two-way sign in front of you, turn left. The woodland path now levelling out passes by a log seat on the right and beyond the trees also on the right, you will see the buildings of Stonedelf House.

Coming to an iron kissing gate at a three-way sign, go out into the driveway of Stonedelf and bearing slightly to the right but not walking into the driveway (you will see a gate across it from where you are), walk into the narrow signposted path. There will be a cleared area to your left used for garden rubbish. Then crossing over a wide track the gateway into Stonedelf will again be on your right. Walk into the opposite path, then coming to a three-way sign, turn left onto a descending path, which will soon bring you to a bridge. Turn left over another bridge where you will be forced to turn right and go up a gravel path, which will climb up and pass by a brick building on the right. Coming out into more open ground the buildings of The Grange at Warninglid, will be in front of you. With an iron gate and two-way sign in front of you, turn right onto the footpath, which will run parallel with the road on your left for some way before it crosses the driveway of Lyndhurst and continues on the opposite side. Coming to an iron gate you will now have to join the road. Turn right, but as quickly as possible cross the road to use the grass verge there to continue the short way into Warninglid where, on coming to the crossroads, the *Half Moon* is in front of you.

To continue the walk and with the pub on your left, carry on down The Street, the road going south through this charming village. Very soon with Herrings Cottage and a footpath sign on the left, turn left into a driveway. Then with a house and barn in front of you, bear right onto a grassy path and going between a timber garage and power line pole, go over a stile at a gate. Allotments are on your left and shortly beyond go out into a cultivated field. With a hedge to the right, walk on down the headland on a wide grassy path. Go over a stile set in a hedge then, coming to an iron kissing gate, go through it and bear left. An iron fence and hedge will be on your left, continue along by it. Go through a second iron kissing gate. Then going by an area overgrown with rhododendrons, you will go through a third kissing gate, still with the iron fence and trees on your left. The wide grassy track will come to a gate, go over the stile and with a bungalow, Paddocks Farm, in front of you, turn left onto the road.

With the bungalow now on your right, turn right into its garage driveway and in only a few steps turn left to go across a stile set in the hedge. The stile is inscribed 'Charles and Diana 1981'. Walk half right across this field and go over the stile set in a fence. Now with hedge and fence on the left, the headland bearing left will come to a stile. Go over it then across a plank over a ditch. You will then have to negotiate two unique stiles either side of a farm track! Now in a paddock and with a hedge on your right, the headland will continue through a series of small paddocks and over other stiles, the last of which will have a waysign. Going through a gate with a three-way sign in front of you, turn left onto a farm track.

With Southgate and Portways Farms and a two-way sign on your right, bear left to go through a wicket gate at a cattle grid. Continue now down a metalled lane, going through another wicket gate and coming out onto the B2115 road. Turn left, cross over the road and, with houses on the left and just beyond one called 'Coldharbour', turn right at a waysign, going over a stile into a large field. On the other side and facing you are some trees and a main grid pylon. Walk across the field to the pylon and coming to the trees at a two-way sign, go over a stile into the wood. On your right through the trees you will see the structure of the pylon. In a very short distance you will come out into an area which contains three very large beech trees. Bear to your left and with these trees on your right, walk on beyond them and cross over a dry ditch. You will see the clear path continuing through an area of bracken. Go over a plank bridge and stile at a two-way sign into a large field. A fence is to your right whilst in front of you is a large modern building and barns.

Follow the fence down the field to a two-way sign then bear away slightly to your left, away from the fence. Now with the modern building much closer, you will see a gate set in a line of trees. Go over the stile and across a railway sleeper bridge and with a two-way sign on the right, come out onto a wide track: *Note*, there has been a footpath diversion here. You now turn right onto the track to turn left in a few metres (note the white sign nailed to a tree here) into a wide grass path going between paddock fences. With a two-way sign and stile on the right, cross the bridge in front of you. Then go over the stile at a gate on your left (ignoring the other gates here). With a hedge on the right, walk up this headland to the next gate and going over the stile there, continue on a wide grass track.

To your left is a large modern chalet bungalow. A little further on, and on the right, you will go by some of the buildings of Slaugham Place Farm. You are now on a metalled lane, which goes through an area containing large buildings. On the left is a large lake. When you come to a two-way sign, turn left onto the lakeside path. You will pass by a building on your right. Now go over a railway sleeper bridge and with a two-way sign in front of you, turn right. This narrow enclosed path will come to a stile; go over it and you are in Slaugham churchyard with the car park beyond.

UPPER DICKER AND MICHELHAM PRIORY

WALK 25

★

5.5 miles (8.8 km)

Maps 1 : 50.000 scale 199. 1 : 25.000 scale TQ 40/50

What a splendid day out this walk makes, and combining it with a visit to Michelham Priory, 'offers a treat rarely to be met with in the South of England' (not just Sussex you will note) (*History of Sussex* 1870). The original Priory, commenced in 1229, took 100 years to complete and had a very chequered existence. It was finally dismantled around 1537 and rebuilding began in 1587 by the Pelhams. The building is now owned by the Sussex Archaeological Society. The entire history of the buildings is, of course, contained in the guide book. The house and grounds are open daily from March 25th–October 31st (11 am–5.30 pm) and Sundays only February, March and November (11 am–4 pm); there is an admission charge. An added attraction is the fully restored and operational watermill which mills flour every Wednesday. An easy walk, almost flat, with some good views of the Downs, although I should warn you that two sections of the route over bridle tracks can be very muddy in the winter.

Upper Dicker is accessible from the A27(T) north of Alfriston or from the A272 via the A267 south from Heathfield. On reaching the village turn into the junction signposted Arlington and Hailsham; this is opposite St Bede's (The Dicker) School at these crossroads. In only about 5 metres there is a large layby on the south side of the road, opposite The White House and Merlyn's School of Motoring (1991). The location for this park and start point is GR(199)551097.

From the layby walk back to the crossroads and turn left. Keep to the left hand roadside grass verge and continue on past a bungalow on the left, Shermans Oak. Just beyond the *Plough* pub on your right, turn left and go over a waymarked stile (WW = The Wealdway), into a field used as a caravan site. With a hedge on the right, follow the two field headlands around to the next waymarked stile at a gate. Bear right over the stile into a field, passing by at first on the right a house and garden. Then with hedge and trees on your right, continue on this headland to the trees in front of you, Park Wood.

Where the hedge and woods meet, go over a waymarked stile. Park Wood is now on the left with a field to your right. Walk on down this headland and shortly a building will appear, part of Park Wood Farm. You will be forced out into the farm track, turn left onto it. The house will be on your right; just beyond the house turn right over a waymarked stile at a gate. Walk across this meadow to a gate in the hedge in front of you, the left hand post is waymarked. Now in another field, you should note that two fields away

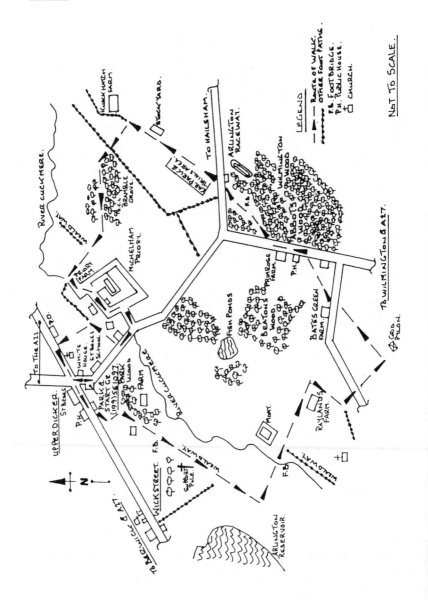

there are four individual oak trees. Using the left hand one as a marker, walk towards it and you will then see your next waymarked stile set in the hedge. Be careful—there is a long drop on the other side. On the far side of this narrow meadow, walk to a single oak tree and just beyond it go over a timber footbridge; you are now in the field containing the four oak trees. Walk across the field to pass by the one in line on your right and continue on beyond it to a timber power line pole. Endeavour to keep this at a distance of about 15 metres to your right. A short way beyond the pole you will then have a hedge on your left; continue on to a gateway in the opposing hedge in front. The river Cuckmere will now be quite close by on your left.

Go through the gateway; a disused stile is here. Now you will follow a clearly marked grass farm track over this field which will lead to another gateway. Go through it and in only a few paces beyond turn left and go over a large foot (and horse) bridge across the river Cuckmere. *Note*: this is the first of two bridleways which can be muddy. This path enclosed by bushes will go by a waymarked stile on the right, and going under main grid power lines will then emerge onto a farm track. Bear left onto it and you will shortly go by Raylands Farm on the right. Now on a metalled lane, go beyond the farm buildings to turn right off the lane at an oak waypost marked 'Alfriston'. Go over the sleeper bridge and stile. With a hedge on the left and farm on the right, go over the next stile into a field. The hedge will still be on the left. Walk up the headland and go through a gateway in the hedge in front into a field—a hedge will now be on the right. In about 60 metres and coming to trees in which you will see a marker post showing the Weald Way continuing ahead, our intended route turns left across the field. In only a short way across this field a gate will come into view in the hedge. Go through it and turn right onto a lane and just before reaching a gate on your left, turn left to go over a stile which is partially hidden in the hedge here.

With the hedge on the right, walk down this rough headland and reaching the bottom of the field keep close to the hedge on your right. In the corner made by the other hedge in front and well concealed in it, are two stiles with a plank bridge between. Coming out into a large field walk directly ahead of you across the field to a main grid power pylon which is beyond trees and a hedge in front of you (not to be confused with a grid pylon to your right). Keeping the pylon just to your right you will see your next stile in the hedge as you approach it, which as you will find is a twin stile with planks between which you should take care crossing.

Now in a very rough, overgrown field, bear left and walk across it and you will be approaching a hedge to your front in which you will see a wide gap spanned by a collapsible wire fence. Beyond the hedge to your right you will see a building. Go through the collapsible gate into a large field and walk across it to the hedge on the far side. At about half way bring the hedge and fence on your left closer to you. This will bring into view a wide gap in the hedge in front, spanned as before by a collapsible gate—go through it into another field, on the other side of which you will see two redundant stiles. Walk into the wide track between them and go through double gates onto a lane. Walk straight across it, going through the gates of Bates Green Farm.

Now on a concrete road, walk straight ahead through the farm. When beyond the last of the buildings, continue on the stone track and coming to a gate, go through it. Turning left, then right through another gateway you will then have a hedge on your right. Walk down the headland of this field to the trees and hedge in front. Go through a makeshift gate in a fence and just beyond go over a stile into a field. Bearing slightly to the right, go through a gap in a line of trees to the front, a house is in the corner of this field on your right. Once through the gap and now in a small field, bear half left. You will see a building beyond the hedge on your left. Coming to a gate in the corner of the field, go through it and turn left onto a road. Now, on your left will be the *Old Oak Inn*.

Walk on up the road passing Primrose Farm on the left. In about 200 metres beyond the farm, go by on the right a Forestry Commission entry way into Abbots Wood. Then with a gateway on the left and shortly beyond, turn right off the road into what is clearly a bridleway. (This is the second section of bridleway which you might find muddy). This fairly narrow path will continue to a horse bridge. Go over it and you will come out into a clearing and turn left—all very confusing with a number of tracks and paths going every which way, but not to worry; you simply walk the length of the clearing (north) towards a line of timber power support poles and power lines, to reach a point where you are following a track with the poles on your right. In a short while the track will lead you under the power lines and the poles will then be over on your left. Shortly beyond you will emerge from trees and be facing a house, here go across the road and turn left into the metalled lane, opposite the house, leading to Knock Hatch Farm.

First you will pass by on the left a large field car park and trials area. Continue on up the lane to a brick built stockyard on the right. You will see Knock Hatch Farm buildings ahead of you in the trees. About 150 metres beyond the stockyard turn left off the lane, going through a gate into a field. Bearing a quarter left, walk across it to a line of trees on the far side in which, as you approach, you will see a stile. Go over it and turn left onto a farm track and in a few paces turn right to go over a stile at a gate. Here the East Sussex Authority, who normally have a cavalier approach to waymarking, have provided both a concrete waymarker and an oak marker post directing the way to Michelham. Now in a large field with the woods of Bramble Grove on the left, continue on round this headland. You will be forced to turn left over a waymarked stile into the woods, shortly going over a collapsed sleeper bridge.

This delightful woodland path continues past an oak marker post on the right, then going over a plank bridge and suddenly coming to a waymarked stile, go over it into a meadow. Walk across the short distance to a Weald Way marked gate and go through it into a narrow meadow. The Cuckmere river will be on your left, beyond which you will see the buildings of Michelham Priory. Coming to the end of the meadow, turn left and go over the river bridge. Now on a farm track and passing a marker post on the right, continue straight ahead between the large modern barns of Michelham Priory Farm. Just beyond the farm buildings and on your left is the imposing gateway into the priory.

The walk continues down the priory lane and you will pass by on the left the lovely old watermill, where shortly beyond you will come out onto the road. Turn right, passing the Dower House on the right. Walk on up the road and at the entrance to a farm track, turn right into it. There is a marker post here directing to Hailsham with a stile on the right. Bear left through a gate into a field, making for a timber power line support in front of you. On reaching it bear left to a gate set in a fence, on the other side of which is a waymarked stile. Go over it and walk straight across the field following a clear track to a line of trees in front—go over two stiles and plank bridge between.

Once again follow a clear grassy track across this field to the buildings (Upper Dicker) in front of you and, going over a stile between houses, the path continues to a quadrangle of houses, village shop and post office. Turn left and left again onto the road and pass Holy Trinity church on the left. Just beyond you turn left at the crossroads to rejoin your motor car.

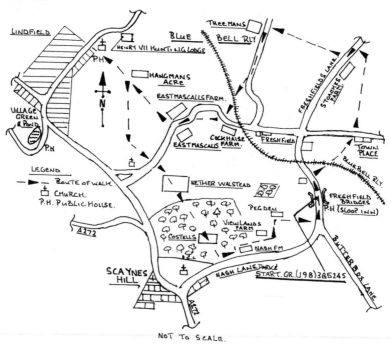

LINDFIELD

BLUE BELL RLY

TREEMANS

HENRY VII HUNTING LODGE

P.H

HANGMANS ACRE

EASTMASCALLS FARM.

FRESHFIELDS LANE

STONCHES FARM.

FRESHFIELD

N

VILLAGE GREEN & POND

COCKHAISE FARM.

EASTMASCALS FARM.

TOWN PLACE

P.H

BLUE BELL RLY.

LEGEND
→ ROUTE OF WALK
✠ CHURCH.
P.H. PUBLIC HOUSE.

NETHER WALSTEAD

PEGDEN

FRESHFIELD BRIDGES
P.H (SLOOP INN)

A 272

VIEWLANDS FARM

COSTELLS

NASH FM.

BUTTER BOX LANE

SCAYNES HILL

NASH LANE PARK
START. GR. (198) 385245

A 272

NOT TO SCALE.

FRESHFIELD BRIDGES AND THE BLUEBELL LINE

WALK 26

★

10 miles (16 km)

Maps 1 : 50.000 scale 198. 1 : 25.000 scale TQ 22/32

This delightful walk will certainly have some surprises in store for you. Not only does it go through some beautiful countryside, but the buildings along the way are superb. Lindfield is a photographer's paradise and I have routed the walk so that you might call at the beautiful old church and its close neighbour, Henry VII's Hunting Lodge (circa 1390). You may possibly have to stand aside to give a wave to the stream trains of the Bluebell Railway (as my wife and I did) and receive a whistle in return.

There is nothing difficult about this walk over undulating farm and woodland. The paths are good even though we did this walk after 24 hours of rain. Similar to the Ardingly walk, No 20, I would advise you to avoid the South of England Show period, usually the weekend between the first and second weeks in June.

Freshfield Bridges is north of Scaynes Hill which is east of Haywards Heath both, of course, on the A272 cross country road. To reach the start point, turn north at Scaynes Hill into Nash Lane. A service station is on the corner here and you will then go by the church on your left. Coming to a fork, turn left into Freshfield Lane (the right hand fork is Butter Box Lane) and in only a few hundred metres the *Sloop Inn* will be on your right. Just beyond the pub are two river bridges. There is adequate road verge parking between them on either side of the road. The location for parking and starting this walk is GR(198)385245.

Walk up the road to pass by the entrance of Freshfield Mill Farm on the right. Continue on the short distance with two houses on the left, Freshfield Mill Cottage and The Millers. Just beyond at a field gate on the right, go over a stile and turn left. Climb another stile on the left and up on a bank, just beyond, is a two-way sign. Here go over yet another stile and the path continues into a large field. In front of you is a line of trees in which, from where you are, is a distinctive gap. As you approach you will see the bridge over the Bluebell Line. Go over the gate, a permanent fixture at this end of the bridge. Crossing it you will come out into a meadow. With a fence now on the right, walk on down the headland. Town Place Farm will be over to the left with Town Place in front of you. Coming then to a timber fence, go over a stile and continue down the headland with a hedge on the left. At the bottom of this field are two gates with a bridge between. Go over the two stiles; there is a two-way sign on the left past the second gate. Bear left and go over a third stile set in a wire fence and with the fence on your right (it will end after a short way) walk across the field to a line of trees ahead. On

107

the left hand end of the line are two very large oak trees beneath which, as you pass them by on your right, is a two-way sign. Walk on down this headland, passing another two-way sign on the right. Beyond the trees on your right is Town Place. You will pass by, also on the right, a third waysign. Rounding a corner made by the trees, go through a gateway and turn right after coming out onto a lane.

Town Place is now in front of you. Walk on by the buildings and, just before leaving the last of them, turn left off the lane, into a wide track across a large field. At the beginning of the track, down in the grass, is a concrete waysign. With a fence on the right walk the length of this field and, reaching the end of it, go over a stile. The path continues into the wood ahead of you and through the distinctive gap in the trees. The woodland path was intended to go over a stile, which is now ruined and has long been by-passed. The way through the wood is quite clear. Emerging from the wood the path continues along a field headland with trees to the left and towards another line of trees in front of you. On reaching them, go ahead through a gap and turn left onto a metalled farm track which will, very shortly, come to a road, Freshfield Lane.

Turn left onto it, passing on the right the entrance way into Latchetts. Please make sure you use the road side grass verge to continue on down the road, and very soon you will come to a waysign on the right. Turn right and going up an embankment, turn right again at a two-way sign. Here on your right will be a nursery of young trees with the buildings of Latchetts beyond. The descending headland will come to a two-way sign. Turn left onto a wide track across a cultivated field. Coming to a two-way sign, on your left, the track now continues into woods and will shortly come to a crossing track. Walk ahead, then with a two-way sign on the left, turn right; go over another crossing track. On the left is an area of newly planted hardwoods.

At the next two-way sign on the left, turn right and the descending track goes over a railway sleeper bridge beyond which is a two-way sign. Turn right—a building will be on your left. The track now descending steeply comes to a footbridge. Go over the bridge, cross over a rubble track and continue into the opposite grassy path climbing, at first, and going by on the left power support poles. At a crossing track with a two-way sign on the left and a shed on the right, continue to a gate. You will be able to go around its left hand post. With a three-way sign on the left, the path now goes out into a field. Continue on its headland—there is a hedge to your left. You will pass by an estate house on the same side. Continue the short way beyond it and coming to a gateway, turn left and then right onto a gravel driveway. On your right is a waysign where you turn left onto Treeman's Road. In only a few paces you will pass, on the right, the entranceway into Treemans and stables.

Continue down the road—*please keep to the right*. Passing a massive oak tree on the right and shortly beyond and on the same side, there will be a concrete waymarker. Turn right and go over a stile. The path goes through a newly planted copse, on the other side of which go over a stile, set in a wire fence, into a field. Walk over to another stile in a fence to your left. Now in a meadow set out as a jumping course, bear to your right to a gate at a two-way sign. Go over the stile and walk towards a timber fence, going over the new stile set into the fence at a waysign, go around a clump of trees on your left. As you do so you will come to a fence on the right. Where it comes to a corner, walk on beyond it and with it at your back, walk half right across this meadow to a corner formed by hedges. Go over the stile set in a fence. Then go over a single plank bridge, bearing left to go over another stile and with a two-way sign just beyond, go up an embankment and cross over the Bluebell Railway line. Please observe the notice!

Go down the opposite embankment over a stile and a footbridge. A narrow path continues through trees—on your left is a dyke. Coming to a stile at a two-way sign, go over it and through the steel gate and over the bridge in front of you. On the other side of the bridge, bear right and with trees and hedge on your right continue up the wide headland farm track. Coming to a steel gate, go over the stile. A waysign is on the right. Turn right on to a dirt track and in a few paces turn left onto a farm track. Continue on down to a road; buildings will be in front of you.

Turn right onto the road and as soon as possible cross over to the left hand side to avoid a dangerous bend. There are houses now on either hand. Coming to the bend walk off the road bearing left and you will have farm buildings to left and right. Walk on to a fence beyond them and at a two-way sign go over a stile. The path continues across a large field. A small building is in this field, walk towards it, passing it on your right, to the left will be first one and just beyond it a second oak tree. There will also be widely spaced fence posts on to which you should now converge. Where this fence bends to the left, follow it round—trees will now be in front of you. On reaching them, go over the stile; the narrow path now going through woods (watch out for obstructions on the ground along here) comes out onto a road—turn left and again across over to the right hand side.

Continue on the road, passing on the right the entrance to Paxhill Park Golf Course and on the left the lovely old building of East Mascalls. Walking on down the road, you will pass various other buildings including East Mascalls Farm on the left. Just beyond, go over the road bridge across the river Ouse where, on the right at the other end, is a concrete waymarker. Turn right and this will bring you onto the wide headland which will follow the course of the river for some way on your right. (You might catch a glimpse of a kingfisher if you're lucky). You will eventually come to a two-way sign on your right. Turn left where a broad track goes across the field to a line of trees. Go over a footbridge into a field. A fence will be on your right, as will Hangman's Acre Farm. Walk up the headland and coming to a gate and three-way sign, cross over the concrete trackway into the farm on the right and continue into the opposite path. Now, coming to a two-way sign, turn right at a large oak tree on the left. This narrow path will come to a stile; go over it and you will come out into an enclosure of houses.

Walk ahead, in front of you now is the Lindfield church, All Saints. Could I suggest that before paying a visit, you bear right at the church into a lane with a brick pavement which will then bring you to the beautifully preserved hunting lodge of Henry VII, which regrettably is not a public building. Return to the church on the same lane and turn right into the churchyard. This building is really worth a visit. To continue into the village walk out of the churchyard and continue down the street beyond what was once *The Old Tiger* inn. All the pubs are dispersed along its length, with the village pond and green at the other end.

To continue the walk, return back to the church and retrace your steps back over the last stile to return to the entrance into Hangman's Acre Farm. Having reached this point and with the three-way sign and gateway in front of you, turn right onto the concrete farm road. Coming to a bridge, go over it and continue beyond the steel pipe barrier across the lane. Further down the lane at a two-way sign, turn left. Go over a stile at two gates; the narrow path between fence and hedge leads into a wood. Go over a footbridge, the buildings to the left, beyond the trees are Great Walstead School and farm. The narrow path continues between trees and hedges, then at a two-way sign, the path will emerge from the trees onto the entrance drive into the school and Walstead Farm (a public right of way). Turn right into the driveway and walk on down to a road.

Cross over the road and go over the stile opposite at a two-way sign and walk across this field to the opposite stile. Go over it and the stile opposite across the lane (the entranceway to Walstead Manor). Now with a large oak tree on your left, walk on across the field to another large oak tree. You will also see buildings beyond the trees and hedges in front of you. Just beyond the second oak tree at a two-way sign, go over a stile set in the hedge. You will find yourself on a driveway and in the garden of the house immediately on your left Hindover Cottage with another house over on your right. Walk between these buildings and with a timber garage on your left, go over another stile set in a hedge. Bearing to the right, go over yet another stile at a gate into a field across which the clear path continues to a field gate. Go over this stile into a large field.

The way across this field will at first go by a fence on the right, then on your left out in the field will be a small area of newly planted trees. Keeping these on your left, continue across the field to a wood in front of you. You will then see a two-way sign at the edge of the wood. Go across a footbridge here and down some concrete steps. The path now goes through woods, then at an old ruined gateway, is a three-way sign—turn left.

After some way and coming out of the woods and at a crossing track, with a power line pole on the right, turn left. The track again continues into woods and for a short way you will go by other power line supports. However, the track will draw away from these and will now be over to your right. Then coming to a fork at a three-way sign on the left, turn into the left hand branch. The way continues into a broad grass tree lined track with paddocks to left and right. Coming to the metalled driveway of Costells, turn left onto it. This will take you by the front of this lovely building. Both it and its continuing gardens will be on your right, passing stables on your left. Costells drive will go through a gateway—walk on. Still on a metalled lane and just before it makes a junction with a road, turn sharp left at a two-way sign on your right.

Along this metalled driveway (all these driveways are public rights of way) very shortly Yew Tree Cottage, a large house, will be in front of you. Bear right, go over the stile at a gate and two-way sign in front of you. The path now goes across a field and with a hedge on your left, walk towards a large house, Nash Farm, and its tennis court. Just beyond at a two-way sign, go over a stile at a gate into a meadow. Walk diagonally across to the opposite corner and go over the stile there into an enclosed path which, in only a few metres, will come to a two-way sign on the left. Turn right into a field and with a hedge on the right, walk to a gateway in the hedge in front. Once again, walk to the diagonally opposite corner of this field, on the left then will be Viewlands Farm. With a two-way sign in the field corner, go over a stile. Watch out for the few steep steps down to the lane. Turn left, with Nash House on the left and with a two-way sign here, the lane bears right. Continue to another farm in front of you and just before reaching these buildings, turn left at a two-way sign into an enclosed path, which at first goes over a series of stepping stones. Continue on into a wood, and emerge to be facing a fence and two-way sign. Go through the large aperture in the fence. Walk down this field to a power line pole surrounded by a fence in front of you. On reaching this point, turn right and now with a continuing fence on your right, walk on to trees in front of you. Then go over a gate, bearing immediately left on to a clear woodland path.

With a large oak tree on your right, the obvious well-worn track bears round to the left in these woods, to emerge facing a paddock fence. Turn left and with the fence on your right, continue by it. Then reaching several gates at a three-way sign, with a stable on the right, go through the gate on your left into a paddock; Ham House Stud is on your left. Walk again diagonally to the opposite corner of this paddock, and go over the stile at the waysign, then turning right onto a driveway.

Walk on the short distance to a road, Freshfield Lane and turn left. On your right is *The Sloop Inn* and just beyond is your car.

DITTON PLACE AND STAPLEFIELD

WALK 27

★

6.5 miles (10.4 km)

Maps 1 : 50.000 scale 187. 1 : 25.000 scale TQ 22/32

This beautiful rural walk has some marvellous distant downland views. The terrain is undulating and there is nothing more taxing than two fairly steep sections of possibly 150 metres in length close to the start and finish points. There are some fairly long stretches of quiet lanes and farm tracks, which are firm and dry. Even after the heaviest day's rain in 30 years (June 1991), we encountered nothing that our boots could not withstand. Staplefield's church, St Mark's, is a mere youngster, built in 1847, but it is nevertheless well worth a visit. The interior of the church is a delightful surprise and in no way Victorian.

Staplefield is quite easily reached by the major road systems which surround it but you will find that the starting and parking point, just north of the entrance into Ditton Place School in Brantridge Lane, is very remote and you should be careful to ensure that you have parked in the correct place, which has safe road verge parking. This is 100 metres north of the entrance into Ditton Place School and on the east side of Brantridge Lane, on a bend with good views of the road in both directions. It is further identified by being opposite a field gate (not used by farm traffic). The location of this point for parking and starting is GR(187)288298.

From your parking spot, walk back (south) down the lane to the school entrance and here on your left is a footpath sign. Go over the stile here, which brings you into a large clearing in the surrounding woods (Northland). With trees on the left, walk away from the stile and in 40/45 metres, and bearing slightly to the left, walk into the narrow path, the course of which is fairly distinct and not to be confused with a wide track—not a right of way—which goes off to the right. Almost immediately the path will descend quite steeply towards a deep ravine and here the path will turn sharply left. This ravine, the course of a stream, will be on your right. In only a few metres the path will be at the top of a series of steps down the side of the ravine. Go down them and across the footbridge over the stream, one of many tributaries feeding the source of the river Ouse in this area.

Climbing up the opposite set of steps you will come out into an open area and here turn left onto a wide track. Coming to a two-way sign in front of you, turn right and climbing up the short steep section of track, go over a stile at the top of the rise, set in a wire fence to come out onto the clear area of a plateau with trees on the left, Bury Wood. After about 300 metres, turn left into the wood and here almost hidden in the trees is a two-way sign. Go over the stile and walk directly ahead, ie follow the direction of the sign, still

112

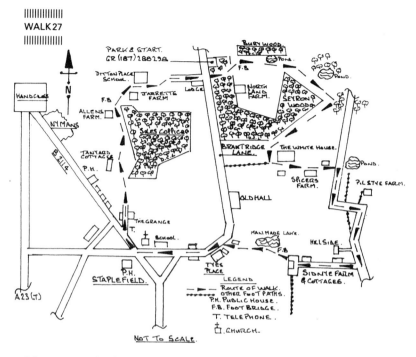

with trees on the left and open grassland on the right. From here the Wealden views will start to unfold.

Soon along the line of trees on the left, you will pass by, also on the left, a pond. Still keeping the trees close at hand, continue on round this headland and shortly beyond the pond you will come to a gate, stile and three-way sign at the edge of the wood. Continue on by them, on your left. The path continues through a narrow section of trees then, coming to a stile, go over it and a second one only a short distance away. Still with the trees on your left, continue along the headland and, coming to a two-way sign at the abrupt end of the wood, bear right at the sign onto a broad grassy track. The views now extend to the left and right. Walk on to the two-way sign in front of you. On reaching it, turn right but bearing over to the trees on your left. On reaching another pond on the left, in the trees, walk diagonally left across the field to its opposite corner. From here you will see the next footpath sign under the trees across this field.

As you get nearer you must bear to the left of the sign to go over a stile set in the fence. Turn right onto the farm track and walk back the few metres to the sign and turn left. The path continues now into Seyron Wood. Along the length of this path are set large slabs of stone. The woodland path is then restricted by the continuing woods on the right and a barbed wire fence on the left. You will be walking towards farm buildings. The path will then emerge into a barn yard and turn right at a two-way sign onto a farm track. The barn and other buildings beyond will be on your left. Continue on the farm track and you will see as soon as you turn the next corner, the considerable extent of the White House Farm complex.

Continuing down the track and coming to a metalled crossing lane at a three-way sign, you turn left to continue the walk. (You should note, however, that here if the weather has turned foul, you can turn right and walk back to the junction with Brantridge Lane and turn right onto it. You will be with your car in about ¾ mile). Having turned left there will very soon be a thatched garage on your right and here bear right off the metalled lane onto a gravelled one. On your left is a duck pond and the large half-timbered building of The White House is on the right. Continue on down the lane and going through a gateway it will ascend gently to Spicers Farm with a two-way sign on the left, the stone track is now paved with concrete. After some way and with a large red brick house on the left, the farm track makes a junction with a lane, opposite which is a pond.

Turn right, with the lane then bending to the left and then right. You should, at this point, look up to your left and on top of the bank, almost hidden by a tree, is a two-way sign. A short cut footpath goes into the field on your right. This cuts off the next corner of the lane. It follows a fence on the left, but if the crop and grass has not been cut in this field and it is wet, I suggest you continue still on the lane. Doing so you will go by the entrance into Pilstye Farm on the left. A little further on and just before going over a bridge and on the right will be a footpath sign. This, of course, is where you would have rejoined the lane had you used the short cut across the field.

The lane having passed by the entrance on the right to Hillside starts to climb and where it levels out, turn right into the signposted track to Sidnye Farm. Passing the first of Sidnye Cottages on the right, number 71, and then after some way coming to numbers 72 and 73, walk into the farmyard just beyond these cottages. Continuing into the yard and with the white painted farmhouse directly in front of you bear right to a two-way sign at a gate. The farm house will be on your left.

Go through the gate into a field. The farmer has provided a path across the field (which had been laid down to oilseed rape in 1991) and almost immediately a very large man-made lake will come into view on the far side. The path will descend to a footbridge. Go over it and with a two-way sign at the other side, bear left. The narrow path now goes through thickets and other vegetation.

To the left is the deep cut stream whilst on the right is the high bank of the lake hiding the water. Coming to an area of fairly open ground, follow close by the wire fence now on your right. Soon you will be forced to bear left into trees beyond which you will be in a cultivated field. Turn right onto the headland, a line of trees will be on your right. Follow this long headland to a two-way sign. Tyes Place and other buildings are beyond the trees. Go over the stile here and you will be in a garden. Walk across it to the forecourt of the house to your front and turn left onto it and now simply follow the driveway of the houses to its junction with Brantridge Lane. Turn left onto it.

Continue on the lane and soon there will be houses to the left and right. Then, coming to a road junction, bear right, signposted to Staplefield and Slaugham. With St Mark's church and the village school on the right, continue to Staplefield crossroads beyond which is *The Victory* inn. The walk continues by turning right at the crossroads, signposted Handcross and Crawley. You should from this point be able to see the sign of *The Jolly Tanner* pub further up the road. Walk on to a public telephone kiosk and at the footpath sign here, turn right into a lane. Post Office Cottages will be on the left, where shortly beyond and on the right is The Grange. From this point until the next landmark, no other directions are required than to follow the twin tracked concrete lane.

Tanyard Cottages will be on the left and, coming then to a three-way sign and cattle grid on the left, turn right to still follow the twin tracked lane through a gateway. Shortly beyond and coming to a junction with another track at a three-way sign, turn right. There is also a sign here, 'Allens Farm'. Follow this concrete lane and just before Allens Farm, turn right at a two-way sign. Go up a flight of steps through a wicket gate into a field; a hedge and Allens Farm will be on your left. Go through a gate in front of you. Now almost directly under the grid power lines and at a two-way sign, turn left through a gate and over a sleeper bridge. As directed by the footpath signs, follow the two headlands of this field to another gate, stile and two-way sign. Go left over this stile and you will now be following a delightful woodland path. A steep ravine is on the right. At the next two-way sign bear right and the descending path comes to a footbridge. A huge oak tree is laying across the path here, but there is plenty of head room.

Go over the bridge. The path climbs gently away from it and with the stream now on your left, comes out into partially open ground. You will come to a fork and take care to bear right into the climbing track which for a short distance will be fairly steep and will come to a pole gate at the top of the rise. Go through the gate into a field. On your right is Jarretts Farm and in front of you is the magnificent building of Ditton Place.

Bear right and with the farm's timber fence close by on your right, walk along its length to a gate set in the fence. Go through it and turn left onto the driveway of the farm, whose buildings will be on your right. Passing a house on the right the farm driveway will merge with the Ditton Place drive and here bear right. The imposing front aspect of Ditton Place will be in full view. Walk down the drive and at the lodge, on the right, turn left onto Brantridge Lane. There on the road verge is your car.

||||||||||||||
WALK 28
||||||||||||||

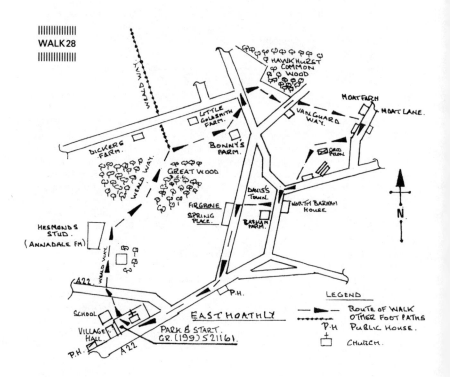

NOT TO SCALE.

EAST HOATHLY

WALK 28

★

5 miles (8 km)

Maps 1 : 50.000 scale 199. 1 : 25.000 scale TQ 41/51

'This parish is remarkable in the district for its pleasant village street, and the number of excellent residences which it contains', wrote Mark Lower in 1870. With the A22 running through the village, the former is no longer true, but the latter statement regarding the 'residences' still remains, albeit no longer single residences.

From the church the walk goes north to Hesmonds Stud, a very plush modern establishment, formerly Annadale Farm, from where you will continue along the Weald Way, a long distance path. The route then turns east to Bonny's Farm and Moat Farm, then back south to East Hoathly. A very pleasant mixed farm and woodland walk over lovely rolling Weald country which, in the main, has good firm paths and tracks. The old church is a great attraction.

As you will see, the A22 trunk road runs through the village. Very conveniently the walk starts from the large car park, signposted off the A22 and bordered by the church, school and village hall (and right behind the *Forresters* pub!). The car park is free, the location is at GR(199)521161.

Go into the churchyard, noting what a magnificent lychgate it has, and with the porch entrance on your right, walk on by the church down the metalled path towards the school. Leave the churchyard through a wicket gate; the school is now on your left. This path will lead to a gap between trees, turn to the left. A cultivated field will be on your right with trees to the left. Then at a three-way sign on the left, which is also marked WW (The Weald Way), go over the stile and turn right onto a broad grass track between paddock fences. Coming to a gate, go over the stile and across the A22 road into the metalled driveway opposite, where there will be a concrete waymarker. This drive leads to Hesmonds Stud, going by various dwellings on the way, the last of which, a large converted oast house, is on the right. Just beyond, the stud stables and other buildings will be in sight. Continue on the metalled drive which will shortly go through the brick entrance pillars, with the plaque 'Hesmonds Stud', and into the stableyards.

Having passed by all the stable buildings, continue out of the yards onto a concrete paved track which will have paddock fences on either hand. Where the concrete ends there will be two wide grass tracks separated by a big hedge facing you. Be sure to walk into the left hand one with the hedge and a ditch on the right. Continue on past a gate on the left, beyond which there will be paddocks contained by timber fences. Where this track levels out take a breather; turn around and you will get a good view of the Weald from here to the Downs beyond.

117

Continue along the track and, coming to a hedge and woods (Great Wood), go by a waymarked stile and across a plank bridge into a field. Trees will be on your left on the far side of this short stretch of field. Go through an old gateway and the way continues on a woodland track, a great place for foxgloves in summer. Then, coming to a waymarked stile, go over it to come out into open ground. Bear slightly to the left and go under main grid power lines and make for the stile which is in sight. As you will see this is waymarked—go over this stile into a large field. Be sure to follow the direction of the last waymarker, ie bearing to the right. As you progress you will see your next stile situated at the corner of the wood and which, as you approach, will be waymarked stiles with a plank bridge between—go over this into a field. You will pass under power lines (not main grid) and walk towards a single oak tree in the field to a hedge beyond.

Go through a gap in the hedge. On the other side of this field you will see Bonny's Farm, which has been in sight for some time. Walk across the field to it and again at a single oak tree in this field, turn left and walk to a fence close to the building. Provision has been made in the fence (close to the house and garden) for walkers to pass through it. Make for the gate in the hedge on the other side of this field and go through it, turning left onto a lane.

A short way up the lane you will see a three-way white road sign. On reaching it, turn right through a wide gap into a large field, where you should make a 45° turn to the right to walk to the south-east corner of this field. As you progress across it (thus bringing the trees of Hawkhurst Common Wood closer) to your left you will see in the south-east corner, the roof of a building and a timber power line support; there you will find an old gateway with wire stretched across it. Go out onto the lane and the house is in front of you—turn left and walk up the lane. Go by the entrance to Windrush on the right and another gate on the same side, then a gate on the left. Just beyond, turn right into a wide grass track between hedges. This is a section (not waysigned) of the Van Guard Way. Beyond the hedges, with a modern bungalow and garden on the left and field on the right, follow this headland down to a gap in a hedge and turn immediately left. In this field a tall wide hedge is on the left. Follow this headland to reach another hedge facing you and in the corner here formed by the two hedges go through a squeeze gate (two timber uprights) which is well concealed. Turn right. Now with a hedge on the right, walk down this field headland and turn left; trees are now on the right.

In only a few metres along this headland turn right through a gateway, one post has a waymarker, then through a ruined steel gate and over a railway sleeper bridge across a stream. On the other side and facing you are two beech trees; one has a twin trunk. Walk between the trees and you will be in a rough field. Walk ahead up the rising ground with scrub wood and a fence on the left. You will be able to detect a track and still with the bushes, trees and fence on the left, walk on up the rising ground—the trees on the left. You will see buildings (Moat Farm) beyond the trees on the left. You will find that as you proceed the going gets rougher and can be wet and muddy in winter, especially under the gate that you next go through into Moat Farm. Here walk over to the 'gate' in front of you, go over the stile, coming out onto Moat Lane and turn right.

Walk on down the lane past the entranceways into Covert and Greenways and both entranceways into Badgers on the right. Just beyond, on the same side, is a postbox, then another entranceway and about 30 metres beyond this, again on the right—turn right through a white painted metal gate. You are now in a rough sloping meadow and you will see in the next field, beyond trees in front of you, a grid power pylon. Keeping this to your front, walk towards it. You will be walking towards the trees and, coming to a stile, go over it. The path continues into a section of woods; at this point for a time you can no longer see the pylon. The path descends and bears left to a timber footbridge across a stream.

Now in a large meadow and with trees, hedge and stream on your right, follow these around the headland. Go by a gateway and on a rough field track, now on your right are three animal drinking troughs. Continue ahead to a gateway in sight in a hedge. On reaching it, turn left. The hedge is on the left, and there in front only a few paces away, is a new stile and the landmark pylon is back in sight. Go over the stile into a large field and walk towards the pylon. You should pass it by on your left, making for the corner of the field formed by hedges. Just beyond it farm buildings will appear, beyond the hedge to the left. Go over the stile in the corner and turn left, and beyond the trees on your left you will see the farm buildings. Walk on down this headland to the next stile. Go over it and you will be walking alongside the farm beyond the hedge on your left and towards a modern house on the same side. Still on a headland, go past the house and just beyond, on the left, is a clump of trees contained by a new chain link fence. As soon as you can, get down to this fence and where it ends, turn left. Go down an embankment and over a new stile. Turn right onto a road, you will see a concrete waymarker here.

Walk up the road to the junction and bear left into the left hand fork, signposted 'East Hoathly ¾'. With the entranceway into North Barham House on the left, turn right at a concrete waymarker at a stile beside two brick pillars. Go over this stile and now in a field, Barham Farm is on the left, and a hedge on the right. Parts of this field can be wet and you may have to retreat to slightly higher ground to your left. But in any event, walk the length of this field and, going through a gap in a hedge, continue into the next field. The original hedge will still be on your right. Go over the next stile and turn left onto a lane.

With a red brick estate wall on the right, continue on by the entranceways into Firgrove and Spring Place. This pleasant lane will continue on for about ¾ mile and then it makes a junction with a road. Bear right into it, signposted 'East Hoathly and Eastbourne'.

As soon as possible cross over the road to continue on the left hand side pavement into East Hoathly, now only a short way away. Passing the *Kings Head* pub, continue on and you will join the A22 road. A short way beyond that junction, you turn right, across the A22, into the entrance of the car park. Before you turned into it you will, no doubt, have seen *The Forresters* pub just beyond.

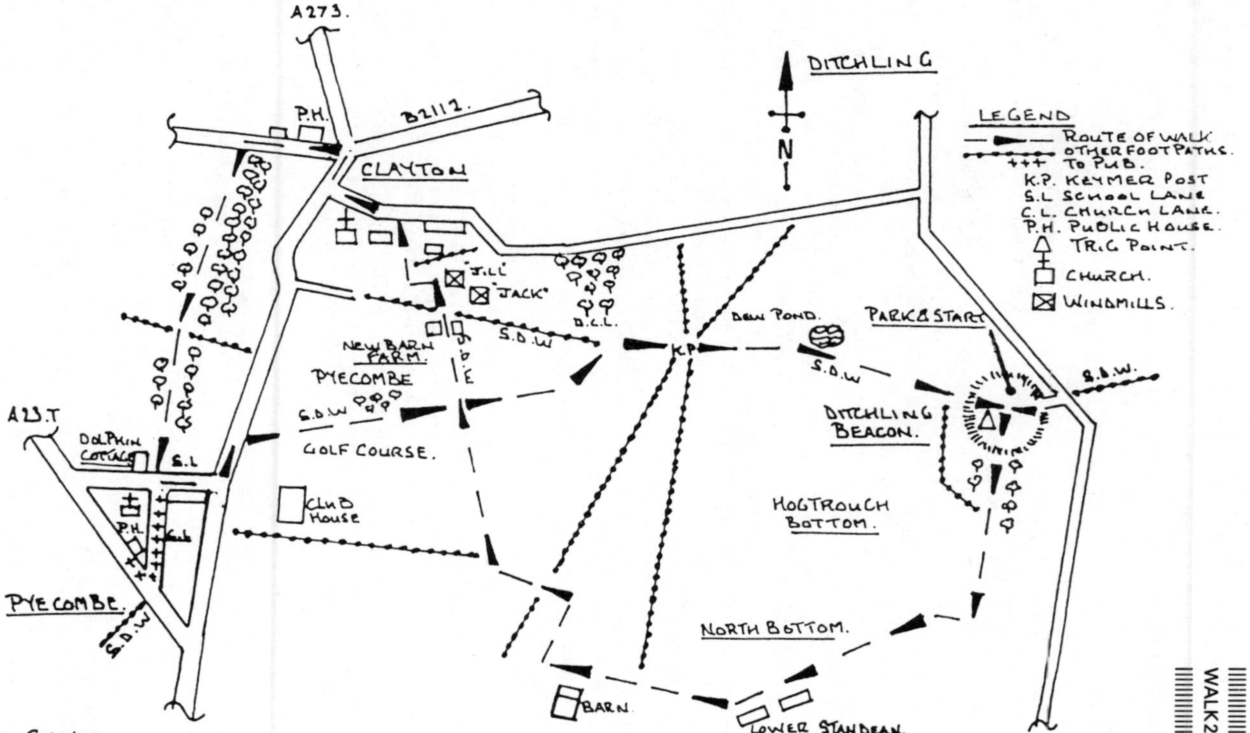

NOT TO SCALE.

WALK 29

DITCHLING BEACON

WALK 29

★

7.5 miles (12 km)
or
5 miles (8 km)

Maps 1 : 50.000 scale 198. 1 : 25.000 scale TQ 21/31

Ditchling Beacon ('the roof of Sussex') at 816 ft (248 m) is a spectacular place to start a walk from and it just gets better as the walk unfolds before you. This is by no means a strenuous walk, but there are long climbing stretches. As with Walk 18, I have to advise you that because of the exposed nature and elevation of the terrain, you should choose your day with care and according to forecast. As you will see from the alternative distances quoted you would, for whatever reason, be able to cut the walk short at Clayton Windmills and return to the Beacon car park via the South Downs Way, but I hope that this would not be the case. I do assure you that you would not want to miss a visit to the beautiful churches of Clayton and Pyecombe, not to mention the pub(s)! But whichever length of walk you choose, both will take you to the Clayton windmills, 'Jack and Jill', with Jill being open to the public on Sundays only, May–October and between the hours of 11 am to 4 pm.

To attempt to direct you by road to Ditching Beacon would take more space than I have available. Suffice to say it is about equi-distant between Haywards Heath and Brighton and above Ditchling village. The walk starts from the National Trust car park on the Beacon at GR(198)332132.

From the car park walk west on the South Downs Way. Ditchling village is below you on your right. In a very short distance on the left is the Beacon trig point and a marker post. Turn left, this clearly defined path at first going through an area of blackthorn trees and a fence on the right goes out onto open downland. The Brighton to Ditchling road is on your left. The field path will take you to a two-way sign; turn right onto a wide track which will very soon bring you to a gate and three-way sign. Go through the wicket gate and turn left. Going down this track you will have caught a glimpse of 'Jack and Jill' on the skyline to the right. The descending track comes to another gate, on the left is a three-way sign and marker post. Go through this gate and bear right, keeping away from the fence and blackthorn trees on the right.

Walk in the cleft of the valley formed by downland on either side, and go through a steel wicket gate at a marker post. Now aim to keep a middle course over the downland between trees on either side; there is a sheep track for you to follow. Quite soon you will come to a fence and, bearing to your left, make for a field gate in it—one of its posts being a marker. Go through the wicket and turn left. The fence is now on your left; then with another marker post on your left, bear right onto a climbing stone farm track. The buildings of High Park Farm will be to the left.

This track will bring you to a wicket gate—again one of its posts is the waymarker. Go through the gate bearing left, still on the stony track. Soon the buildings of Lower Standean Farm will appear to your left. With one of the buildings close by on the left and marker post on the right, turn right onto another farm track leading to a three-way sign and marker post on the left. Go through a gateway. The stony track continues towards a barn and stockyard. Passing these on the left, with a marker post on the right, the track makes an acute bend, and continues on to a six-way sign and marker post on the left. Ignore gateways to left and right—carry straight on with a blackthorn hedge on the left.

Passing an old ruined wicket gate and two-way sign on the left, bear right. The hedge is now on the right and a fence on your left. A two-way sign is ahead of you, at which you turn left. Now still with the fence on the left, walk on to the next three-way sign and turn right. The fence continues on the left, also with blackthorns. The windmills will have been in full view. The descending track will now have Pyecombe golf course on the left. After a short, sharp climb the track comes to a four-way sign—carry straight on into the South Downs Way. Directly ahead will be New Barn Farm and just beyond, Jack and Jill.

Go through a gate and The Way continues through the farm with timber fences on either hand. Coming to a gateway with a South Downs Way marker post on the right, bear left to continue the few metres to the windmills. *Note* If you do not wish to continue on to Clayton and Pyecombe, you can, after your visit to Jack and Jill, simply turn back to the last marker post, go through the gate and walk back along The South Downs Way to Ditchling Beacon.

Should you wish to continue then, on leaving the windmills, turn right and walk the length of the car park, turning left at the end. With waymarkers here, go through a wicket gate onto downland. A fence is on the left and below is the village of Clayton, including your next landmark—the church.

Coming to a three-way sign at the corner of the fence, bear left and this will put you onto an obvious path descending through bushes to a steel wicket gate. From here the continuing path, at one point very steep, comes out onto the village road. Turn left and in only a few metres you will come to the magnificent lychgate of the church. This will whet your appetite to see other treasures inside the building, including its wall paintings.

On leaving the church, walk on the short way to the junction of the A273 road. Turn right onto it and, as soon as possible cross over the road to the pavement opposite and continue over the railway bridge where, just beyond, you turn left into a metalled lane. *The Jack and Jill* pub is on your right and you can gain access to it via its garden entrance. The walk continues on up the lane and then, passing a bungalow, Wolstonbury, on the right about 200 metres further on, turn left into a signposted bridle track. This is the only place on the whole of this walk where you might require good footwear. This pleasant woodland path climbs up Wolstonbury Hill, passing a National Trust placard, then a three-way sign on the left and wicket gate down on the right. Continue straight on up the hill. Passing a three-way sign and stile on the right, the path which has levelled out into the open will come then to a crossing track. Another National Trust placard and three-way sign are on the right. Go over the track into the path opposite.

This also is a woodland path, which will, along the way, pass by a four-way sign and stile on the right. Then going through an old wicket gate, the path eventually comes out among the houses of Pyecombe, then continues the short distance to have Dolphin Cottage on your right. Now at a crossroad, the church is over to your right and is unusual in that you enter the churchyard through a centre pintle swing-gate; Coombes church at Lancing is the only other example that I know of. Despite this church not having such distinctions as wall paintings, it is nonetheless a lovely, peaceful old place, and I'm sure you will be glad you made the extra effort to visit it. If you decide to use Pyecombe's pub, then walk down Church Lane and *The Plough* is on the right, but I would advise that you then return back up Church Lane from the pub, to avoid walking on the busy A273 road.

Turning right into School Lane, walk down to its junction with the A273 road and turn left, not onto the road but a bridleway/footpath which has been created. You will have noted at the church you are now on the South Downs Way! This footpath will lead to a South Downs Way sign directing you across the road into the entranceway to Pyecombe golf club. Walk up the drive to the car park area and The Way bears to the left, continuing at first between fences across Pyecombe golf course on a stony track. You will still be in sight of Jack and Jill. Going by a blackthorn thicket on the left and again with fences on either hand, the track reaches a gate that you should recognise—New Barn Farm—and the windmills are to your left. Go through the gate, on the right is a four-way sign including the South Downs Way. Cross into the bridle track opposite which will continue for some way over cultivated downland. On reaching a marker post, go through a steel wicket gate and turn left with a fence on your left. The path will make a junction with the South Downs Way. Turn right onto it, in a few paces you will pass the South Downs Way marker post on the left and still the views continue!

Passing by on the left both keymer posts and five-way signs, The Way goes on across the downland, going through two wicket gates and passing a dew pond on the left. You will then have only ¾ mile to make the most of the views before reaching the Beacon car park and the ice-cream van which is usually stationed there!

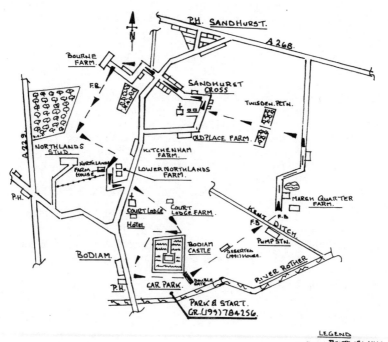

P.H. SANDHURST.

A 268.

BOURNE FARM.

SANDHURST CROSS

TWISDEN. PLTN.

F.B.

OLD PLACE FARM.

NORTHLANDS STUD.

KITCHENHAM FARM.

NORTHLANDS FARM HOUSE.

LOWER NORTHLANDS FARM.

A 229

P.H.

MARSH QUARTER FARM.

COURT LODGE

COURT LODGE FARM.

KENT DITCH

F.B

F.B

HOTEL

BODIAM.

BODIAM CASTLE

PUMP STN.

DESERTED (1991) HOUSE.

RIVER ROTHER

P.H.

CAR PARK.

DOUBLE GATE

PARK & START.
GR. (199) 784256.

LEGEND
— ▶ — ROUTE OF WALK
∿∿∿ OTHER F/PATHS
C.P CAR PARK.
P.O POST OFFICE
P.H PUBLIC HOUSE
✝ CHURCH.
F.B. FOOT BRIDGE.

NOT TO SCALE.

BODIAM

WALK 30

★

5.5 miles (8.8 km)

Maps 1 : 50.000 scale 199. 1 : 25.000 scale TQ 62/72 and TQ 82/92

There is a special attraction in this eastern edge of Sussex, which clearly has some influence from Kent in the profusion of oast houses and hop gardens. A lovely walk, at first across flat farmland, small areas of woodland and the attractive hamlet of Sandhurst Cross and its beautiful old church. It is at this point you will change direction to return to Bodiam Castle. This magnificent moated building, now owned by the National Trust, was built in the incredibly short time of four years, 1385–1388, by Sir Edward Dalyngrigge on instructions from Richard II to keep the French at bay! The interior was sadly dismantled in 1644, and finally saved by our old friend 'Mad Jack' Fuller (Walk 23), who purchased the remains in 1829 to prevent a local builder from demolishing the entire remaining structure for its stone block content. But no doubt you will purchase the booklet published by the National Trust which contains a well written history of the castle and Bodiam.

To reach Bodiam we choose to use the A272 and the A265 from the west. Access from north and south is via the A229 or A28 and from the east on the A268. Park in the National Trust car park; a charge of 50p is levied by the Trust. The walk starts from this location at GR(199)784256. I would advise that you park at the start of the fence, which will be on your left and facing the castle.

You will have noted that a stone track goes through a gateway in the car park, which you will join to continue the short distance to a three-way sign. Take the signposted direction 'To the Castle' which, of course, is to your left. Make sure that you keep to the stone track, which very soon will take you through double field gates. This mile long track, first going by a deserted (1991) house on the left, will then reach the 'Kent Ditch' pumping station. Here you use a footbridge to cross the 'Ditch' to its other bank, where you turn right to then go over a gate on the bank at a two-way sign only a few feet from the bridge. Once over the gate, no doubt you will find it locked, turn left. Now on your left in this large field is another ditch. In front of you on the far side of the field is another footbridge, go over it. At its other end the step is marked with the usual yellow plastic waymarker used by East Sussex County Council and which I shall simply refer to as 'waymarkers'.

The direction of the path continues across the meadow. You should head towards a main grid pylon to your left, then coming to a gateway go through it; one of the posts has a waymarker. The pylon is now directly in front of you, as is Marsh Quarter Farm. Walk across this rough meadow and keep

125

the farm to your front as you approach its perimeter fence, while to your left is a stile with a waymarker. Go over the stile and now among the farm buildings continue out of the farm on the track which will go by a pond on the right. Coming to a junction turn left onto the continuing track, almost immediately going by a barn and modern house on the right (Little Marsh Quarter) where, just beyond and on the left, turn left to go over a steel gate. (We, in fact, went round this obstacle, which no doubt you will be able to do unless you are lucky enough to find the gate repaired!). There is a concrete waymarker here at the gate. You will now be in a cultivated field across which the farmer has taken the trouble to leave a wide footpath through the crop (you will encounter this again several times). The path heads towards Twisden Plantation. Go over the stile, the path continues through the wood and you will leave it by another stile. Continue on a wide footpath across a cultivated field. Sandhurst Cross hamlet and church are now in sight. Go over another stile by an old tree stump. The path continues now across a meadow, bearing half right and heading towards a single large oak tree. Go over the stile there and turn left into a cultivated field, similarly provided with a wide path through the crop. Old Place Farm is on your left.

Coming out onto a lane, turn right. The church and buildings of Sandhurst Cross are on the left. Coming to a junction your route bears right; here could I suggest that you walk the short distance to visit the ancient church of St Nicholas, after which your way continues by more houses of the hamlet to come to a junction with the Sandhurst to Bodiam road. With the road direction signs on the left, cross over the road into the opposite lane, signposted to Hawkhurst. The lane shortly will bend to the right. A bungalow here is on the right—continue ahead into a farm track signposted 'Ives Cottage and Bourne Farm'. A concrete waymarker on the roadside is here on the left.

The descending stony track goes by a large modern house on the left (Tippens), then with Ives Cottage on the right the track continues on. Bourne Farm will appear to the front. Turn left off the track and going through a field gate, with waymarkers on both posts, walk down this meadow to go through a gateway. A hedge and hop garden will be on your right. Continue along this headland and, coming to a gate on the right, go over it. One of the posts has a waymarker. Once over the gate, turn left, which will bring you into the hop garden with a stream on the left. Shortly beyond the gate, go over a footbridge on your left; a waymarker is on the step. The path continues straight across a cultivated field to a gateway. Its left hand post has a waymarker. Now with Barn Field Wood on the right, walk up the headland. With the wood still on the right, but now with another wood also to your left at a crossing track, carry straight on up the rising farm track. Ignoring a track going down from the left and with Northlands (an Arabian stud) in front of you, continue towards the buildings. On your right there will be a fence, the corner post has a two-way marker—turn left here.

The farm track now heading towards a wood will pass by trees on your right. Reaching a crossing track, go over it—the deeply rutted track now ascends between fences, which give way to only a hedge on the left. A little further on there will be trees also on the right. You will then come to Lower Northlands Farm; go through a wicket gate set in a fence. To your right is

Lower Northlands farmhouse. Now on a metalled farm lane, continue for about ½ mile to make a junction with the Bodiam to Sandhurst road. There will be a footpath sign on the left, turn right onto the road.

In only a few metres there will be an old Sussex timber-faced cottage on the right. Turn left across the road and go through an old gateway into a field. Bearing slightly to the right, walk up this field towards a single huge oak tree on the other side. As you approach it you will see a gate, on the left of which is a stile. Go over it and turn left. There is a notice, one of several, directing you onto the footpath—Court Lodge Farm, stables and paddocks are close by. Now with trees and fence on the left, walk along the edge of this paddock and coming to the other end of it, turn right. On reaching a timber fence, go over the stile and, crossing over a concrete track, the path goes up a grass bank. On your right will be the entrance gate leading into other paddocks. Here will be other buildings, also on the right, with oast houses. Bearing now to the left, go through a double gateway and turn right.

This path, going by the buildings and paddocks on the right, will descend down this headland, from where you will get a marvellous view of Bodiam Castle. Then, going over a stile at the bottom, you will be in the castle grounds. Here, to make the walk completely circular, we turned right and went between the museum and the causeway entrance to the castle. The car park appears all too quickly.